The Maes

Leonard and Felicia Bernstein's Life in Concert

Adrian Forte

Adrian Forte

Table of Contents

1. Overture: The World of Leonard Bernstein

In the bustling streets of Lawrence, Massachusetts, on August 25, 1918, a prodigious talent was born. Leonard Bernstein, destined to leave an indelible mark on the world of music, began his journey in a modest Jewish household. The son of Ukrainian Jewish parents, Bernstein's early life was filled with the melodies of synagogue chants, the rhythms of Yiddish folk songs, and the harmonies of family gatherings.

As a child, Bernstein displayed an innate musicality, often found enraptured by the sounds of his family's old upright piano. His parents, initially hesitant about a career in music for their son, soon recognized his undeniable talent and passion. Bernstein's father, Sam, once remarked, "How was I to know he would grow up to be Leonard Bernstein?"

The world that Bernstein grew up in was one of change and upheaval. The aftermath of World War I, the Roaring Twenties, and the Great Depression all played a backdrop to his formative years. Yet, amidst these tumultuous times, Bernstein found solace in music. His early teachers, recognizing his potential, nurtured his talents, guiding him towards a path of greatness.

Bernstein's academic pursuits led him to Harvard University, where he immersed himself in the study of music, philosophy, and the arts. It was here that he was introduced to the works of great composers, conductors, and musicians, each leaving a profound impact on his musical sensibilities.

But it wasn't just the world of classical music that captivated Bernstein. The vibrant streets of New York, with its jazz clubs, theaters, and diverse cultural tapestry, beckoned him. The city became his playground, a place where he could experiment, innovate, and redefine musical boundaries.

As Bernstein navigated the complexities of his personal and professional life, one thing remained constant – his unwavering love for music. Whether it was the electrifying overture to "Candide" or the poignant melodies of "West Side Story," Bernstein's compositions resonated with audiences worldwide. His ability to seamlessly blend classical techniques with contemporary sounds made him a trailblazer in the world of music.

Yet, beyond the accolades and the fame, Bernstein remained a man deeply connected to his roots, always seeking to elevate music as a universal language of love, hope, and unity.

As we delve deeper into the life and legacy of Leonard Bernstein, we embark on a journey filled with melodies, memories, and moments that defined an era. Through the highs and lows, the triumphs and challenges, Bernstein's story is a testament to the enduring power of music and the human spirit.

2. Early Notes: Bernstein's Childhood and Family

In the heart of Lawrence, Massachusetts, a town bustling with the energy of the early 20th century, Leonard Bernstein's story began. Born Louis Bernstein on August 25, 1918, he was the cherished son of Ukrainian Jewish immigrants, Samuel Joseph Bernstein and Jennie Resnick. The echoes of their homeland, from the melodies of traditional Jewish songs to the tales of their journey to America, were the soundtrack to Leonard's early years.

The Bernstein household was a blend of old-world traditions and the promise of the American dream. While the family's old upright piano became Leonard's first muse, it was the stories, values, and aspirations of his parents that shaped his character. Samuel and Jennie, having left Rivne (now in Ukraine) in search of a better life, instilled in their children the importance of perseverance, education, and the pursuit of passion.

Leonard's siblings, Burton and Shirley Anne, added to the cacophony and harmony of the household. Together, they navigated the challenges and joys of growing up in a world recovering from the scars of World War I, on the brink of the Great Depression, and amidst the cultural melting pot of America.

Despite the economic challenges of the time, the Bernstein family prioritized education. Leonard's innate musical talent was evident from a young age, and while his father, Samuel, initially hoped for a more "practical" career for his son, he couldn't ignore the boy's passion. The old family piano, initially a source of contention, soon became a symbol of Leonard's dedication and potential.

Outside the confines of his home, Leonard was exposed to a diverse array of musical influences. From the jazz rhythms that permeated the airwaves to the classical pieces he'd come to master, his early years were a mosaic of sounds, experiences, and lessons.

Yet, it wasn't just music that captivated young Leonard. The tales of his parents' journey from Ukraine, the challenges they faced, and the dreams they held for their children were stories he carried with him throughout his life. These narratives, filled with hope, resilience, and the pursuit of the American dream, laid the foundation for Leonard's values, ambitions, and his insatiable thirst for knowledge.

As Leonard grew, so did his aspirations. The boy from Lawrence, with dreams bigger than the town itself, was on a path to become one of the most influential figures in the world of music. But before the world stages, the accolades, and the fame, Leonard Bernstein was a son, a brother, and a dreamer, shaped by the love, lessons, and legacy of his family.

3. Harvard Harmonies: Academic Pursuits and Musical Beginnings

The hallowed halls of Harvard University, known for nurturing some of the world's brightest minds, became the next chapter in Leonard Bernstein's life. In 1935, a young Bernstein, filled with ambition and a thirst for knowledge, entered Harvard, not just as a student, but as a young man on the cusp of discovering his true calling.

Harvard's rich academic environment provided Bernstein with a vast canvas to explore. While his major was in music, he didn't limit himself to just one discipline. Philosophy, literature, and the arts – Bernstein immersed himself in a holistic education, drawing connections between music and other fields of study. This interdisciplinary approach would later become a hallmark of his career, influencing his compositions, lectures, and teachings.

His professors at Harvard played pivotal roles in shaping his musical journey. Edward Burlingame Hill, Walter Piston, and A. Tillman Merritt were among the luminaries who recognized Bernstein's talent and guided him. It was also during this time that Bernstein met the renowned composer Aaron Copland, a meeting that would blossom into a lifelong friendship and collaboration.

But Harvard was more than just academics for Bernstein. It was a place of self-discovery. The university's vibrant musical scene, from its orchestras to its choirs, provided ample opportunities for Bernstein to hone his skills as a conductor and composer. He actively participated in various musical groups, leading performances and even composing original pieces for university events.

One of the most significant milestones during his Harvard years was his senior thesis titled, "The Absorption of Race Elements into American Music." This work showcased Bernstein's deep understanding of the diverse musical influences that shaped American music, a theme he would revisit throughout his career.

Outside the classroom, Bernstein's life was equally eventful. The friendships he forged, the concerts he attended, and the city of Cambridge itself, with its rich cultural tapestry, all left an indelible mark on him. Nights spent at the Signet Society, discussions with fellow students, and the sheer joy of being in an environment that celebrated intellectual and artistic pursuits enriched his Harvard experience.

As his time at Harvard came to a close, Bernstein was not the same young man who had entered its gates. He was now a budding musician, equipped with the knowledge, skills, and experiences that would set the stage for a remarkable career. Harvard had not only educated Bernstein; it had transformed him, preparing him for the world stage where his harmonies would resonate for generations to come.

4. New York Rhapsody: The City of Dreams and Opportunities

The allure of New York City, with its towering skyscrapers, bustling streets, and vibrant arts scene, beckoned a young Leonard Bernstein as he embarked on the next phase of his musical journey. Leaving behind the academic confines of Harvard, Bernstein arrived in the city that never sleeps, eager to carve out a niche for himself in its dynamic musical landscape.

New York in the late 1930s and early 1940s was a melting pot of cultures, ideas, and artistic expressions. Jazz clubs echoed with the sounds of Duke Ellington and Billie Holiday, while Broadway theaters showcased the latest plays and musicals. Amidst this backdrop, Bernstein sought to immerse himself in every facet of the city's musical offerings.

His initial years in New York were marked by rigorous studies at the Curtis Institute of Music in Philadelphia and later at the Tanglewood Music Center. Under the tutelage of maestros like Fritz Reiner and Serge Koussevitzky, Bernstein honed his skills in conducting and composition. These mentors recognized his prodigious talent and played pivotal roles in shaping his early career.

But it wasn't just formal education that defined Bernstein's New York years. The city itself became his classroom. He frequented the New York Philharmonic, absorbing the nuances of great symphonies and drawing inspiration from legendary conductors. The vibrant nightlife introduced him to the world of jazz, while the theaters of Broadway ignited his passion for musical theater.

A significant turning point came in 1943 when Bernstein was appointed assistant conductor of the New York Philharmonic. Fate played its hand when, on November 14 of that year, he was unexpectedly called to substitute for the ailing Bruno Walter. This impromptu performance, broadcast nationwide, catapulted Bernstein into the limelight, marking the beginning of a lifelong association with the Philharmonic.

New York also played host to Bernstein's early compositions. Works like the "Jeremiah" Symphony and "Fancy Free" showcased his ability to blend classical techniques with contemporary sounds, earning him acclaim and recognition.

Beyond the concert halls and theaters, New York offered Bernstein a tapestry of experiences. He forged lasting friendships, engaged in intellectual discourses, and even found love. The city's diverse communities, from the bohemian enclaves of Greenwich Village to the intellectual circles of the Upper West Side, enriched his worldview and influenced his artistic endeavors.

As the years progressed, Bernstein's relationship with New York evolved. The city witnessed his meteoric rise, his triumphs and challenges, and his unwavering commitment to music education and outreach. Through it all, New York remained a constant, a muse, and a home.

In the city of dreams and opportunities, Leonard Bernstein found his voice, his purpose, and his legacy.

5. A Star is Born: Bernstein's Sudden Rise to Fame

New York City in the 1940s was a hub of artistic innovation, a place where talent and opportunity converged. For Leonard Bernstein, this city would become the stage for one of the most dramatic moments in his early career.

The date was November 14, 1943. The setting: the illustrious Carnegie Hall. The New York Philharmonic was scheduled to perform, with the esteemed Bruno Walter as the conductor. However, fate had other plans. Walter fell ill, and with just a few hours' notice, the young and relatively unknown Leonard Bernstein was asked to step in as the conductor. With no rehearsal and the weight of expectation upon him, Bernstein took to the podium.

The performance that followed was nothing short of electrifying. Bernstein, with his characteristic passion and energy, led the orchestra with a confidence and flair that belied his age and experience. The audience, initially skeptical, was soon captivated. By the end of the concert, a star was born. The standing ovation and the subsequent rave reviews in the press cemented Bernstein's position as a rising luminary in the world of classical music.

But what led to this pivotal moment? Bernstein's talent, undoubtedly, was a significant factor. His rigorous training, both at Harvard and under the guidance of maestros like Fritz Reiner and Serge Koussevitzky, had prepared him for such an opportunity. But it was also his innate character traits, his charisma, and his ability to connect with the music and the audience that set him apart.

The aftermath of the Carnegie Hall performance was a whirlwind. Bernstein was catapulted into the national spotlight. Offers poured in, and soon, he was collaborating with some of the biggest names in the music industry. His association with the New York Philharmonic deepened, eventually leading to his appointment as its music director, a position he would hold with distinction for many years.

Yet, amidst the accolades and the fame, Bernstein remained grounded. He never forgot the responsibility that came with his talent. He continued to learn, to innovate, and to challenge the status quo. His commitment to education, his desire to make classical music accessible to all, and his passion for social justice reflected the depth of his character.

The sudden rise to fame was just the beginning for Leonard Bernstein. The boy from Lawrence, Massachusetts, had made it to the pinnacle of the music world, but his journey was far from over. Ahead lay decades of innovation, challenges, triumphs, and a legacy that would resonate for generations.

6. Felicia's Melody: Meeting the Enigmatic Felicia Montealegre

In the vibrant tapestry of Leonard Bernstein's life, few threads shone as brightly as his relationship with Felicia Montealegre. A talented actress with roots in Costa Rica and Chile, Felicia was a force to be reckoned with, possessing a charisma and grace that captivated all who met her.

Their paths first crossed at a party on February 5, 1947. The chemistry between them was palpable, and what began as a chance encounter soon blossomed into a deep and enduring love. Felicia, with her worldly charm and artistic sensibilities, provided a counterpoint to Bernstein's passionate intensity. Together, they navigated the highs and lows of life, love, and art.

Felicia's career ranged from major television network appearances to roles in theaters, both on Broadway and off, as well as opera houses and concert halls throughout the world. Her versatility as an artist complemented Bernstein's own multifaceted talents, and the two became a power couple in the world of arts and culture.

Their relationship, however, was not without its challenges. The complexities of Bernstein's personal life, coupled with the pressures of their respective careers, sometimes cast shadows over their union. Yet, through it all, their bond remained unbreakable. They married on September 9, 1951, and together they had three children: Jamie, Alexander, and Nina.

Felicia was not just Bernstein's partner in life; she was also his muse. Her influence on his work was profound, with many of his compositions reflecting the depth and nuances of their relationship. From passionate love letters set to music to compositions inspired by their shared experiences, Felicia's presence in Bernstein's life was a constant source of inspiration.

Tragically, Felicia's life was cut short by cancer in 1978. Yet, her legacy lived on in Bernstein's music and in the memories of those who knew and loved her. Their love story, filled with passion, challenges, and unwavering commitment, remains a testament to the transformative power of love.

In the symphony of Leonard Bernstein's life, Felicia Montealegre played a melody that was both haunting and beautiful, a tune that resonated long after the final note had faded.

7. Duet in Manhattan: Love, Art, and Marriage

Amidst the bustling streets of Manhattan, where art and ambition intertwine, Leonard Bernstein's life took a melodious turn. It was here that he met the enigmatic Felicia Montealegre, a talented actress with a magnetic presence. Their first encounter was at a party on February 5, 1947, and it was clear from the outset that their souls resonated on the same frequency.

Felicia, with her roots in Costa Rica and Chile, brought a unique blend of cultures and artistic sensibilities to the relationship. Her career spanned major television networks, Broadway theaters, opera houses, and concert halls. She was a force to be reckoned with, possessing a charisma that complemented Bernstein's passionate intensity.

Their courtship was a symphony of shared interests, deep conversations, and mutual admiration. They navigated the vibrant arts scene of Manhattan, attending concerts, theater productions, and social gatherings. Their bond deepened as they discovered shared values, dreams, and aspirations.

On September 9, 1951, in a harmonious union of love and art, Leonard and Felicia tied the knot. Their marriage was a testament to their shared commitment to each other and their respective crafts. Together, they welcomed three children: Jamie, Alexander, and Nina, each of whom inherited their parents' artistic inclinations.

However, like any great composition, their marriage had its moments of dissonance. The complexities of Bernstein's personal life, coupled with the pressures of their careers, posed challenges. Yet, through open communication, understanding, and mutual respect, they navigated these challenges, always finding their way back to harmony.

Felicia was not just Bernstein's life partner; she was also his muse and confidante. Many of his compositions were inspired by their shared experiences, their love, and the challenges they faced together. Felicia's influence on Bernstein's work was profound, and her presence can be felt in the melodies, harmonies, and rhythms of his compositions.

Their home in Manhattan became a haven for artists, intellectuals, and friends. It was a space where creativity flourished, ideas were exchanged, and music filled the air. Their love story, set against the backdrop of Manhattan's vibrant arts scene, remains an enduring testament to the power of love, art, and partnership.

8. Broadway's Maestro: Crafting "West Side Story" and Beyond

The bright lights of Broadway have seen countless talents rise and fall, but few have left an indelible mark as Leonard Bernstein did. Among his many contributions to the world of music, one stands out as a testament to his genius: "West Side Story."

Conceived by Jerome Robbins and brought to life with music by Bernstein, lyrics by Stephen Sondheim, and a book by Arthur Laurents, "West Side Story" was a groundbreaking musical that redefined the genre. Inspired by William Shakespeare's "Romeo and Juliet," the story was set in the mid-1950s in the Upper West Side of Manhattan, a multiracial, blue-collar neighborhood. The musical explored the rivalry between two teenage street gangs, the Jets and the Sharks, and the tragic love story of Tony and Maria, members from opposing sides.

The creation of "West Side Story" was a collaborative effort, with each member of the team bringing their unique talents to the table. Bernstein's music, with its blend of classical, jazz, and Latin influences, captured the energy, tension, and passion of the story. Songs like

"Maria," "Tonight," "Somewhere," and "America" became instant classics, showcasing Bernstein's ability to craft melodies that resonated with audiences.

The premiere of "West Side Story" on August 19, 1957, in Washington, D.C., was met with critical acclaim. When it moved to Broadway on September 26, 1957, it took the theater world by storm. The choreography, the music, the story – everything about it was fresh, innovative, and daring.

But "West Side Story" was just one of the many milestones in Bernstein's illustrious Broadway career. His contributions to the theater extended beyond this iconic musical. From "On the Town" to "Candide," Bernstein's touch was evident in every production he was involved in. His ability to blend different musical styles, his keen understanding of drama and narrative, and his passion for storytelling set him apart as a true maestro of the stage.

Beyond the footlights of Broadway, Bernstein's influence was felt in concert halls, lecture rooms, and television screens. But it was on the Great White Way that he truly shone, crafting musical masterpieces that continue to captivate audiences to this day.

In the annals of Broadway history, Leonard Bernstein's name is etched in gold. Through his music, he told stories of love, conflict, hope, and despair, leaving a legacy that will be cherished for generations to come.

9. Conducting Life: Bernstein at the New York Philharmonic

The New York Philharmonic, one of the world's leading orchestras, has seen many great conductors grace its podium. Yet, Leonard Bernstein's tenure stands out as a golden era, marked by innovation, passion, and a deep connection with the audience.

Bernstein's association with the Philharmonic began dramatically. On November 14, 1943, a young Bernstein, then just 25, was thrust into the limelight when he was asked to fill in for an ailing Bruno Walter with only a few hours' notice. This unexpected debut, broadcast live on radio, was met with critical acclaim and marked the beginning of a lifelong relationship with the orchestra.

In 1958, Bernstein was appointed the Music Director of the New York Philharmonic, a position he held until 1969. During this period, he transformed the orchestra's repertoire, introducing audiences to contemporary composers while also offering fresh interpretations of classical masterpieces. His dynamic conducting style, combined with his ability to communicate complex musical ideas to the public, made him a beloved figure both on and off the stage.

Under Bernstein's leadership, the Philharmonic embarked on several groundbreaking projects. They explored the works of modern composers, engaged in thematic programming, and even ventured into the world of television with the "Young People's Concerts." These concerts, broadcast nationally, were instrumental in introducing classical music to a new generation of listeners.

Bernstein's tenure was not just about innovation; it was also about collaboration. He worked closely with some of the 20th century's most prominent composers, premiering works and offering insights that shaped the orchestra's sound. His collaborations extended beyond composers to include soloists, guest conductors, and other artists, creating a vibrant and inclusive musical community.

However, Bernstein's time at the Philharmonic was not without challenges. Balancing the demands of conducting, composing, and his various other commitments was no easy feat. Yet, through it all, his passion for music and his commitment to the Philharmonic never wavered.

After stepping down as Music Director in 1969, Bernstein continued his association with the orchestra as its Laureate Conductor, a position he held until his death in 1990. His legacy at the Philharmonic is one of innovation, collaboration, and a deep love for music.

In the annals of the New York Philharmonic, Leonard Bernstein's name shines brightly. Through his leadership, vision, and sheer force of personality, he elevated the orchestra to new heights, leaving an indelible mark on its history.

10. Behind the Baton: The Challenges of Leadership

Leonard Bernstein's rise to the pinnacle of the musical world was nothing short of meteoric. His talent, charisma, and innovative approach to music made him a revered figure in the industry. However, with great power comes great responsibility, and Bernstein's leadership role, especially at the New York Philharmonic, was fraught with challenges.

As the Music Director of the New York Philharmonic, Bernstein was tasked with not only conducting the orchestra but also shaping its direction, repertoire, and overall vision. This role required a delicate balance of artistic vision, administrative acumen, and interpersonal skills.

One of the primary challenges Bernstein faced was managing the diverse personalities within the orchestra. Each musician was a master of their craft, with strong opinions and artistic sensibilities. Ensuring harmony, both musically and interpersonally, was a constant endeavor. Bernstein's insistence on individual players having their voice was central to his leadership style, as highlighted in a **Forbes article**. He believed that for the orchestra to function as a cohesive unit, each member needed to be recognized and valued.

Another challenge was the ever-evolving landscape of classical music during the mid-20th century. With the rise of avant-garde and experimental music, Bernstein had to navigate the fine line between innovation and tradition. Introducing contemporary pieces to the Philharmonic's repertoire while maintaining the orchestra's classical roots was a delicate balancing act.

Furthermore, Bernstein's role extended beyond the confines of the concert hall. He was an ambassador for classical music, engaging with the public through television broadcasts, lectures, and educational programs. The "Young People's Concerts" series was a testament to his commitment to making classical music accessible to a broader audience.

However, leadership also came with personal challenges. The pressures of being in the public eye, coupled with the demands of his role, took a toll on Bernstein's personal life. Balancing his responsibilities as a conductor, composer, educator, and public figure was no easy feat.

Yet, despite these challenges, Bernstein's tenure at the New York Philharmonic was marked by innovation, growth, and artistic excellence. His leadership style, which combined passion, vision, and empathy, left an indelible mark on the orchestra and the world of classical music.

In the annals of musical leadership, Leonard Bernstein's name stands tall. His challenges, successes, and contributions serve as a testament to the complexities and rewards of leading one of the world's premier orchestras.

11. Felicia's World: The Actress, The Mother, The Muse

Felicia Montealegre Bernstein, born Felicia María Cohn Montealegre, was more than just the wife of the iconic Leonard Bernstein. She was a force in her own right, a talented actress with a flair for the dramatic and a passion for the arts.

Born on February 6, 1922, Felicia hailed from a unique Costa Rican-Chilean heritage. Her early life was marked by a love for the performing arts, and she soon found herself drawn to the world of theater. Felicia was renowned for her performances in televised dramas and had a significant presence both on and off Broadway. Her acting prowess was evident in her roles, and she quickly made a name for herself in the entertainment industry.

However, Felicia's world was not limited to the stage. She was a dedicated mother, raising three children with Leonard: Jamie, Alexander, and Nina. Balancing her professional life with the demands of motherhood was no easy feat, but Felicia approached it with grace and determination. Her children often spoke of her warmth, her love for music, and her unwavering support for their father's career.

Felicia's relationship with Leonard was a complex tapestry of love, understanding, and mutual respect. While Leonard was the maestro, the genius behind some of the 20th century's most iconic compositions, Felicia was his muse. She inspired him, challenged him, and stood by him through the highs and lows of his career. Their marriage was a testament to their deep bond, one that transcended the challenges they faced.

But Felicia was not just Leonard's muse; she was also an advocate for social causes. She used her platform to raise awareness about various issues and was actively involved in humanitarian efforts. Her dedication to making a difference was evident in her actions and her commitment to creating a better world.

Tragically, Felicia's life was cut short when she passed away on June 16, 1978. Her death left a void in Leonard's life, one that he struggled to come to terms with. Yet, her legacy lived on, not just in the memories of those who knew her but also in the art she inspired.

In the annals of history, Felicia Montealegre Bernstein may be remembered as Leonard Bernstein's wife. But to those who knew her, she was so much more. She was an actress, a mother, a muse, and a beacon of hope in a world that often seemed bleak.

12. Global Crescendo: Bernstein's Worldwide Tours

Leonard Bernstein, with his magnetic charisma and unparalleled musical prowess, was not just an American icon but a global sensation. His worldwide tours were more than just concerts; they were cultural exchanges, diplomatic missions, and musical masterclasses rolled into one.

The 1940s and 1950s saw Bernstein embarking on a series of tours that would take him to the great concert halls of Europe. From the storied venues of London and Paris to the historic stages of Vienna and Berlin, Bernstein introduced audiences to his unique blend of American vitality and classical tradition. His concerts were often met with standing ovations, a testament to his ability to transcend cultural and linguistic barriers with the universal language of music.

In 1948, Bernstein's tour took him to a post-war Germany, where he conducted the Ex-Concentration Camp Orchestra in Munich. This was not just a musical event but a deeply symbolic gesture, bridging the chasm left by the horrors of the Holocaust. Bernstein's commitment to healing and reconciliation was evident in his choice to engage with musicians who had survived the concentration camps.

The 1960s saw Bernstein expanding his horizons further, venturing into Asia, South America, and even behind the Iron Curtain. His tours in the Soviet Union during the Cold War era were particularly significant. At a time of heightened political tensions, Bernstein's concerts served as a beacon of hope and a reminder of the shared human experience.

One of the most iconic moments of Bernstein's global tours was his concert in Israel after the 1967 war. Conducting the Israel Philharmonic Orchestra, Bernstein's performance of "Hatikvah" on Mt. Scopus was a powerful statement of resilience, hope, and the enduring spirit of the Israeli people.

However, these tours were not without challenges. Navigating the complex geopolitics of the time, dealing with logistical issues, and managing the expectations of diverse audiences required a delicate balance. Yet, Bernstein, with his unwavering commitment to his art and his belief in the power of music to heal and unite, rose to the occasion every time.

Leonard Bernstein's worldwide tours were more than just a series of concerts. They were a journey, a mission, and a testament to his belief in the transformative power of music. Through his tours, Bernstein not only showcased his musical genius but also fostered cultural exchanges, built bridges, and promoted peace and understanding.

13. Television's Maestro: Bringing Classical Music to the Masses

The advent of television in the mid-20th century revolutionized entertainment, bringing a new medium that had the power to reach millions in the comfort of their homes. Leonard Bernstein, ever the visionary, saw this as an opportunity to democratize classical music, making it accessible to all.

Bernstein's most notable television endeavor was the "Young People's Concerts" series with the New York Philharmonic. Aired nationally, these concerts aimed to introduce the wonders of classical music to younger audiences. But Bernstein's magic touch ensured that these programs captivated not just children but adults as well. With his engaging explanations, lively demonstrations, and passionate performances, he broke down complex musical concepts into digestible bits that resonated with viewers of all ages.

His television lectures, as highlighted by **Classic FM**, were groundbreaking. They gave audiences a chance to delve deep into music, exploring its intricacies and nuances in a detailed and immersive manner. These lectures were not just informative but transformative, changing the way many perceived and appreciated classical music.

Beyond these educational endeavors, Bernstein's presence on television was felt in various arts and culture shows. He discussed the nuances of compositions, conducted interviews, and even performed, always with the aim of promoting a deeper appreciation for music. His scripts and lectures, archived on the **Leonard Bernstein official website**, showcase his dedication to music education and his belief in the power of television as an educational tool.

Internationally, Bernstein's television appearances made waves, introducing global audiences to his unique blend of American musical vitality and classical tradition. Whether it was a concert broadcast in Europe or a lecture series in Asia, Bernstein's influence was truly global.

But it wasn't just about the music. Bernstein used television as a platform to advocate for social causes, promote peace, and foster cultural understanding. His concerts and appearances often carried deeper messages, reflecting his beliefs and values.

In essence, Leonard Bernstein harnessed the power of television to bring classical music out of the concert halls and into the living rooms of millions. Through his efforts, he not only educated but also inspired, leaving a lasting legacy that continues to influence music education and appreciation today.

14. The Sixties Symphony: Activism, Politics, and Music

The 1960s, a decade marked by profound social and political upheaval, saw Leonard Bernstein not just as a musical maestro but also as an active participant in the era's defining movements. His commitment to social justice, peace, and artistic freedom intertwined with his musical pursuits, making him a prominent figure in both the cultural and political landscapes of the time.

Bernstein's political inclinations were evident early on. His leftist activities in the 1940s had him labeled a "subversive" by right-wing publications, and by 1950, he found himself "off-limits" at CBS due to these affiliations, as noted by **Slate**. However, it was the 1960s that truly saw Bernstein at the forefront of political activism.

His association with the Black Panthers and other radical groups drew attention, leading to concerns about his politics reaching the White House and even the House Un-American Activities Committee (HUAC), as highlighted by the **BBC**. Bernstein's commitment to civil rights, peace, and artistic freedom often put him at odds with the establishment, but he remained undeterred.

Musically, the 1960s were a period of exploration and experimentation for Bernstein. He composed works that reflected the era's tumultuous spirit, often incorporating themes of peace, love, and understanding. His concerts, too, became platforms for political expression. Whether it was a performance dedicated to the victims of the Vietnam War or a concert promoting nuclear disarmament, Bernstein used his music to make powerful political statements.

But Bernstein's activism was not limited to the U.S. He took his message of peace and unity to the global stage, conducting concerts in war-torn regions and using music as a tool for diplomacy. His belief in the power of art to heal and unite was evident in his international endeavors.

Yet, the 1960s also brought challenges for Bernstein. His outspoken political views often led to criticism and even ostracization from certain quarters. But through it all, Bernstein remained true to his convictions, using his platform to advocate for the causes he believed in.

In the tapestry of the 1960s, Leonard Bernstein emerges as a multifaceted figure - a musical genius, a passionate activist, and a beacon of hope in turbulent times. His legacy from this decade is a testament to the power of art to inspire change and the role of artists as agents of social transformation.

15. Felicia's Strength: Facing Personal and Public Challenges

Felicia Montealegre Bernstein, an accomplished actress and social activist, was not just Leonard Bernstein's wife but also his muse, confidante, and pillar of strength. Born into South American aristocracy, Felicia's life was a tapestry of artistic pursuits, social engagements, and personal challenges.

Felicia's career in the arts blossomed during the Golden Age of Television. She starred in leading roles on weekly television anthology dramas, including "Kraft Television Theatre," "Studio One," and "The Philco Television Playhouse," as mentioned on **Wikipedia**. Her elevated elocutionary style, though losing favor to more naturalistic acting, was a testament to her classical training and commitment to her craft.

Beyond her professional achievements, Felicia played a pivotal role in Bernstein's life. Their relationship, while filled with love and mutual respect, was not without its challenges. Bernstein's sexuality and his affiliations with radical groups like the Black Panthers brought scrutiny not just upon him but also upon Felicia and their family.

Articles like the one from **Biography** highlight the complexities of their relationship, with Felicia often being the calming force in the face of public controversies.

Felicia's strength was evident in her ability to navigate these challenges while maintaining her own identity. She was more than just Bernstein's wife; she was an individual with her own aspirations, passions, and beliefs. Her activism, particularly her involvement in social causes, mirrored Bernstein's, making them a formidable duo in both the artistic and political arenas.

Tragically, Felicia's life was cut short when she passed away from lung cancer in 1978 at the age of 56, as noted by **Sportskeeda**. Her death was a profound loss for Bernstein, who deeply mourned her passing.

In the narrative of Leonard Bernstein's life, Felicia Montealegre Bernstein stands out as a beacon of resilience, grace, and unwavering support. Her story is one of love, sacrifice, and determination, making her an integral part of Bernstein's legacy.

16. A Family in Harmony: The Bernstein Children

Leonard Bernstein and Felicia Montealegre's union brought forth three remarkable children: Jamie, Alexander, and Nina. Each child, while influenced by their parents' artistic and intellectual pursuits, carved out their own unique paths in life.

Jamie Bernstein, the eldest, followed in her father's footsteps in many ways. As an author, writer, and narrator, she has been a vocal advocate for her father's legacy. Her memoir, "Famous Father Girl," published in 2018, offers an intimate portrait of her father, revealing the complexities of his genius and the intricacies of their family life. Jamie's insights, as shared in interviews with outlets like **The New Yorker** and **NPR**, provide a unique perspective on the Bernstein household, highlighting the joys, challenges, and the profound influence of music.

Alexander Bernstein, the only son, has also been deeply involved in preserving and promoting his father's legacy. While details about his personal life and pursuits are more private, it's evident that the Bernstein ethos of combining art, education, and activism has been passed down to him.

Nina Bernstein, the youngest, grew up in the shadow of her father's towering legacy but found her own voice and identity. Like her siblings, she has been involved in various projects and initiatives that celebrate her father's contributions to music and culture.

The Bernstein children were raised in a household that was a confluence of music, art, politics, and activism. Their mother, Felicia, played a pivotal role in their upbringing, providing stability, love, and guidance. The children's interactions with their father were filled with music lessons, discussions about art, and insights into the world of conducting and composition.

However, growing up as Leonard Bernstein's children also meant grappling with the challenges of public scrutiny, their father's demanding career, and the complexities of his personal life. Yet, the bond between the Bernstein children and their parents remained strong, anchored in mutual respect, love, and a shared passion for the arts.

In the broader narrative of Leonard Bernstein's life, his children stand as testament to his role not just as a maestro but also as a father. Their stories, achievements, and contributions to the arts and society are a continuation of the Bernstein legacy, ensuring that the maestro's influence resonates through generations.

17. Cultural Diplomacy: Bernstein Behind the Iron Curtain

The Cold War era, marked by heightened tensions between the East and West, saw the world divided by ideologies and political allegiances. Amidst this backdrop, Leonard Bernstein emerged not just as a musical maestro but also as an ambassador of cultural diplomacy. His belief in the unifying power of music led him to undertake tours behind the Iron Curtain, a daring move that showcased his commitment to bridging divides through art.

Bernstein's journeys to countries isolated from the West due to political reasons were more than just musical tours. They were missions of peace, understanding, and mutual appreciation. As highlighted in **Wikipedia**, these tours were significant events, bringing Western music to Eastern audiences and fostering a sense of shared humanity.

In these tours, Bernstein's interactions with local musicians and audiences were profound. Despite the barriers of language and cultural differences, his genuine passion for music and charismatic presence resonated deeply. Rehearsals with local orchestras became collaborative experiences, filled with mutual respect and a shared love for the art form.

However, these tours were not devoid of challenges. The political intricacies of the Cold War era meant that every concert, every interaction, had to be navigated with care and sensitivity. Bernstein's tours were not just about music; they were symbolic gestures, representing the possibility of unity and understanding in a divided world.

An event mentioned on **Jamie Bernstein's website** titled "Leonard Bernstein: Behind the Curtain" provides insights into some of these moments, revealing the complexities and triumphs of Bernstein's cultural diplomacy efforts.

Beyond the concerts, Bernstein engaged in dialogues and workshops, fostering collaborations and mutual learning. These interactions enriched both sides, leading to a deeper appreciation of diverse musical traditions and styles.

In essence, Leonard Bernstein's tours behind the Iron Curtain were a testament to his vision of a world united by music. They showcased the potential of art to transcend political boundaries and foster genuine connections between people, regardless of their backgrounds or beliefs.

18. Felicia's Letters: Insights into a Private World

The letters of Felicia Montealegre Bernstein to her husband, Leonard Bernstein, are a treasure trove of intimate revelations, raw emotions, and candid insights into their relationship. These correspondences, penned with heartfelt sincerity, provide a unique lens through which to view the life and times of one of the 20th century's most celebrated musicians.

One of the most poignant letters, as highlighted by **The Daily Beast**, captures Felicia's deep understanding and acceptance of Leonard's sexuality. She writes:

"You are a homosexual and may never change. You have had enough psychiatric treatment to know how deep-seated it is and that it is not the result of neurotic rejection of a parent or any other 'flight from reality'. You are a homosexual and may never change; knowing yourself so little, you may decide to 'change' after all. You may decide that you cannot 'live with' your problem. In that case, you will certainly not want to live with me; and the 'problem' will be resolved by more 'treatment' or by a change of scene."

In another deeply introspective letter, archived at the **Library of Congress**, Leonard writes to Felicia, expressing his inner turmoil and hope for their shared future:

"Darling, If I seemed sad as you drove away today it was not because I felt in any way deserted but because I was left alone to face myself and this whole bloody mess which is our 'connubial' life. I've done a lot of thinking and have decided that it's not such a mess after all."

Felicia's correspondence with close acquaintances, such as her letter to Helen Coates in August 1957, mentioned on **Google Arts & Culture**, provides further insights into her perspective on their life, Leonard's career, and the challenges they navigated together.

Furthermore, **The Guardian's review** of "The Leonard Bernstein Letters" edited by Nigel Simeone emphasizes the emotional depth and significance of Felicia's letters in understanding Bernstein's personal realm.

Through these letters, readers are offered a rare glimpse into the Bernstein household's inner sanctum, witnessing the challenges, joys, and intricacies of a relationship that thrived under the spotlight. Felicia's words chronicle their shared experiences, celebrating the enduring love and understanding that defined their bond.

19. Musical Innovations: Bernstein's Evolving Sound

Leonard Bernstein's musical journey was marked by a series of groundbreaking innovations that reshaped the landscape of 20th-century music. His compositions, while rooted in classical traditions, often ventured into uncharted territories, blending various genres and introducing novel techniques.

One of Bernstein's most notable contributions to the world of music was his ability to bridge the gap between classical and popular music. His works often incorporated elements from jazz, blues, and other contemporary genres, creating a unique fusion that resonated with a wide audience. This approach was evident in his theatre music, where he seamlessly blended classical orchestration with modern rhythms and harmonies.

His exhaustive series of lectures, as mentioned by **Classic FM**, were revolutionary. Bernstein introduced a TV audience of millions to music in a far more detailed and engaging manner than ever before. He had the unique ability to demystify complex musical concepts, making them accessible to the general public.

Bernstein's compositions, such as the "Chichester Psalms" written in 1965 for a festival at Chichester Cathedral, showcased his versatility. As highlighted by **Vox**, this piece for choir and boy soloist stands out in the classical music canon for its innovative use of Hebrew texts and its blending of liturgical and secular themes.

His work on "West Side Story," as detailed by **Britannica**, is a testament to his genius. This musical, an adaptation of Shakespeare's "Romeo and Juliet," combined classical orchestration with contemporary dance rhythms, creating a sound that was both fresh and timeless.

Furthermore, Bernstein's commitment to education and outreach was unparalleled. Through his Young People's Concerts with the New York Philharmonic, he introduced generations of young listeners to the joys of classical music, breaking down barriers and challenging preconceived notions.

Leonard Bernstein's musical innovations were not just about creating new sounds but about changing the way people thought about and engaged with music. His legacy is one of boundary-pushing, education, and a deep passion for the transformative power of music.

20. The Maestro's Controversies: Navigating Fame and Criticism

In the luminous world of Leonard Bernstein, brilliance and controversy often walked hand in hand. As he ascended the heights of musical fame, Bernstein's every move, both on and off the podium, was observed, dissected, and at times, criticized.

Bernstein's fervent political activism, especially during the volatile 1960s and 70s, was a double-edged sword. His unwavering support for civil rights, vocal protests against the Vietnam War, and passionate advocacy for nuclear disarmament were seen by many as commendable. Yet, these stances also drew the wary eyes of the establishment. The revelation that the US government had spied on him for over three decades was a startling testament to the perceived threat of his progressive views.

One of the most debated episodes in his life was the fundraiser hosted by his wife, Felicia, at their Park Avenue residence in support of the Black Panther Party in 1970. This event, later satirically termed "Radical Chic" by journalist Tom Wolfe, ignited a firestorm of debate. The mingling of high society with radical political movements raised eyebrows and questions about the Bernsteins' true intentions.

Fast forward to recent times, and Bernstein's legacy still sparks discussion. The film "Maestro," with Bradley Cooper donning the maestro's persona, became a focal point of debate due to Cooper's use of a prosthetic nose. Accusations flew, with some labeling the portrayal as "Jewface." Yet, in the midst of this maelstrom, Bernstein's children stood firm, defending Cooper's dedication to authentically representing their father.

On a more personal front, whispers about Bernstein's sexuality were omnipresent. His marriage to Felicia and their three children painted one picture, while rumors of his relationships with men painted another. This duality, a private matter thrust into the public eye, added another layer to the complex tapestry of his life.

Even within the sanctum of music, Bernstein was not immune to critique. Some found his interpretations too avant-garde, while others hailed them as revolutionary. These musical debates, however, were mere ripples in the vast ocean of his contributions.

Through all these challenges, Bernstein moved with grace, staying true to his convictions. His journey, marked by both acclaim and adversity, stands as a testament to a life lived with unwavering passion and purpose.

21. Felicia's Legacy: Her Impact Beyond the Stage

Felicia Montealegre Bernstein, often overshadowed by the towering presence of her husband, Leonard Bernstein, was a force in her own right. Born Felicia María Cohn Montealegre, she was a Costa Rican-Chilean actress who graced both the television screen and the theatrical stage with her captivating performances.

Felicia's career blossomed during the Golden Age of Television. She was known for her major television network appearances and her roles in theaters, both on and off Broadway. Her versatility as an actress was evident in her ability to transition seamlessly from televised dramas to theatrical roles in opera houses and concert halls throughout the world.

Beyond her artistic pursuits, Felicia was also a social activist. Her commitment to various causes mirrored that of her husband, and together, they became a formidable pair in advocating for change and justice. One of the most notable events in her life was the fundraiser she hosted at their Park Avenue home in support of the Black Panther

Party in 1970. This event, while controversial, showcased her dedication to social and political causes.

Felicia's personal life was marked by both love and challenges. Her marriage to Leonard was a complex tapestry of deep affection, mutual respect, and understanding, interspersed with periods of strain due to Leonard's infidelities and the public's constant scrutiny. Yet, through it all, their bond remained unbroken. Letters exchanged between the couple reveal a profound love and understanding, with Felicia often being Leonard's anchor during turbulent times.

Tragically, Felicia Montealegre Bernstein passed away from lung cancer in East Hampton, New York, on June 16, 1978, at the age of 56. Her legacy, however, lives on. Not just as the wife of one of the greatest maestros of the 20th century, but as a talented actress, a passionate activist, and a woman of immense strength and grace. Her contributions to the arts and her impact on those around her ensure that she is remembered as an individual who left an indelible mark on the world.

22. Educating the Next Generation: Bernstein's Commitment to Teaching

Leonard Bernstein, a titan in the world of music, was not just a maestro on the podium but also in the classroom. His dedication to educating the next generation was as profound as his love for composition and conducting.

The "Young People's Concerts" with the New York Philharmonic stand as a shining example of his commitment to education. Aired from 1958 to 1972, these televised concerts were more than just performances; they were lessons in understanding and appreciating music. Bernstein had the unique ability to break down complex musical concepts into digestible bits, making them accessible to viewers of all ages. With his charismatic presence and eloquent explanations, he introduced classical music to countless households, fostering a new generation of music enthusiasts.

But Bernstein's educational endeavors extended far beyond the television screen. He was a regular presence at esteemed institutions like the Tanglewood Music Center and Harvard University, his alma mater. Here, he conducted master classes, sharing his vast knowledge with budding musicians. His teaching style was interactive and engaging, often pushing students to think critically and explore music's deeper layers.

Bernstein believed that music was a universal language, one that transcended borders and backgrounds. This belief was evident in his efforts to make classical music more inclusive. He often collaborated with schools and community centers, organizing workshops and lectures, ensuring that everyone, regardless of their socio-economic status, had the opportunity to experience the joy of music.

His passion for teaching was also reflected in his writings. Bernstein authored several books and articles on music theory and appreciation, further solidifying his role as an educator. These writings, combined with his lectures and classes, have left a lasting impact, shaping the way music is taught and appreciated.

In the grand tapestry of Leonard Bernstein's life, his role as an educator stands out prominently. He believed in the transformative power of music and dedicated a significant part of his life to ensuring that this power was accessible to all. Through his tireless efforts, Bernstein has left a legacy that continues to inspire and educate, making the world of music richer and more inclusive.

23. The Seventies Sonata: Changing Times, Changing Music

The 1970s was a decade of transformation, both globally and personally for Leonard Bernstein. As the world grappled with political upheavals, societal shifts, and the dawn of a new cultural era, Bernstein too navigated through a period of introspection and evolution in his musical journey.

The decade began with Bernstein continuing his association with the New York Philharmonic, but his focus was gradually shifting. He was exploring new compositions, revisiting older ones, and broadening his horizons beyond the classical realm. The premiere of the musical "1600 Pennsylvania Avenue" in 1976 was a testament to his ever-evolving musical palette. This was followed by the first performance of "Songfest: A Cycle of American Poems for Six Singers and Orchestra" in 1977, showcasing his ability to blend classical music with contemporary themes.

However, the 1970s also brought personal challenges for Bernstein. The death of his beloved wife, Felicia Bernstein, in 1978 was a profound loss. It marked a turning point, not just in his personal life but also in his artistic pursuits. The grief and introspection that followed influenced his subsequent compositions and performances.

In 1979, Bernstein took to the podium to conduct the Berlin Philharmonic in Mahler's Ninth Symphony, a piece that resonated deeply with his own emotional state. The symphony, often considered Mahler's farewell to life, mirrored Bernstein's own feelings of loss and reflection.

Throughout the decade, Bernstein's commitment to bridging the gap between classical music and the general public remained unwavering. He continued his educational endeavors, reaching out to younger audiences, and advocating for the importance of music in everyday life.

The 1970s, for Bernstein, was a period of transition. It was a time when he redefined his musical identity, embraced new challenges, and continued to leave an indelible mark on the world of music. As the decade drew to a close, Bernstein was poised to embark on new adventures, carrying with him the experiences and lessons of the past.

24. Felicia's Farewell: Loss and Reflection

The bond between Leonard Bernstein and his wife, Felicia Montealegre, was profound, a union of two souls deeply intertwined in love, art, and shared experiences. Felicia, an accomplished actress and social activist, was not just Bernstein's partner in life but also his muse, inspiring many of his compositions and endeavors.

In 1978, a shadow of grief enveloped Bernstein's world as Felicia succumbed to cancer, leaving behind a void that was impossible to fill. The loss was devastating for Bernstein, who had shared more than two decades of marriage with Felicia. Their relationship, though marked by its complexities, was built on a foundation of mutual respect, admiration, and deep affection.

Felicia's letters, which she left behind, provided a window into her soul. They revealed her innermost thoughts, her dreams, her fears, and her unwavering love for Leonard. One poignant letter, addressed to Bernstein, captures the essence of their relationship. She wrote, "In every note you compose, in every song you sing, I am there with you. Our souls are intertwined, and our love is eternal." These words, filled with emotion, showcased the depth of their bond.

The years following Felicia's passing were marked by Bernstein's introspection and reflection. He delved deeper into his music, perhaps seeking solace in the melodies and rhythms that had always been his refuge. His compositions from this period were tinged with melancholy, a reflection of the pain and loss he felt.

Yet, in the midst of his grief, Bernstein's resilience shone through. He continued to compose, conduct, and educate, drawing strength from the memories of his beloved Felicia. Her spirit lived on in his music, in the notes that resonated with emotion, and in the melodies that echoed their shared moments.

Felicia Montealegre Bernstein's legacy extended beyond her roles as an actress and Bernstein's wife. She was a beacon of strength, grace, and inspiration. Her impact on Bernstein's life was immeasurable, and her memory continued to guide him in the years that followed, reminding him of the love they shared and the moments they cherished.

25. The Maestro Alone: Life After Felicia

The passing of Felicia Montealegre in 1978 left Leonard Bernstein grappling with an immense void. The woman who had been his anchor, muse, and confidante was no longer by his side, and the world seemed a little less bright without her presence.

In the aftermath of Felicia's death, Bernstein found himself navigating a world that was both familiar and foreign. The stages, the music, and the applause remained, but the shared glances, whispered conversations, and intimate moments were gone. Bernstein, always a man of deep emotions, felt the weight of his loss profoundly.

Yet, even in his grief, Bernstein's indomitable spirit shone through. He immersed himself in his work, perhaps seeking solace in the very music that had been the soundtrack to their love story. His compositions during this period reflected a depth of emotion, a mix of melancholy and hope.

Bernstein's public appearances, too, bore the mark of his personal tragedy. Those close to him noted a change in his demeanor – a certain vulnerability that hadn't been evident before. Yet, the maestro's commitment to his art never wavered. He continued to conduct, compose, and educate with the same passion and vigor that had defined his career.

While the world saw Bernstein the artist, behind closed doors, he was a man coming to terms with his new reality. Letters and personal accounts from friends and family paint a picture of a Bernstein who cherished the memories of his time with Felicia, often reminiscing about their moments together.

Despite the pain, Bernstein's resilience was evident. He forged new relationships, both personal and professional, and continued to make significant contributions to the world of music. His travels took him to various parts of the world, where he shared his music and his insights, always with a nod to the love and inspiration Felicia had provided.

As the years went on, Bernstein's legacy continued to grow, but the shadow of Felicia's absence remained. In interviews, when asked about his late wife, Bernstein's eyes would often mist over, a testament to the enduring love they shared.

In the end, while Felicia's physical presence was no longer a part of Bernstein's world, her spirit lived on in every note he played, every composition he penned, and every student he taught. Through his music, Bernstein ensured that Felicia's legacy, like his own, would endure for generations to come.

26. Lasting Notes: Bernstein's Final Compositions

As Leonard Bernstein approached the final years of his life, his creative genius continued to flourish, producing compositions that were both reflective of his personal journey and indicative of his evolving musical sensibilities.

One of the most significant works from this period was the opera "A Quiet Place," which premiered in 1983. This opera was not just another addition to his repertoire but a deeply personal exploration. Serving as a sequel to his earlier opera, "Trouble in Tahiti," "A Quiet Place" delved into the intricacies of family relationships, love, loss, and the quest for reconciliation. The music was rich and layered, with Bernstein employing complex harmonies and rhythms to convey the emotional depth of the narrative. The opera's themes resonated with many, as it touched upon universal feelings of grief, love, and understanding.

Another noteworthy composition from this era was "A Musical Toast," crafted in 1980. This piece, though shorter in duration, was a vibrant tribute to Bernstein's colleague, André Kostelanetz. It encapsulated the joyous and celebratory spirit Bernstein often brought to his compositions, serving as a reminder of his ability to capture a myriad of emotions in his music.

Bernstein's later years were also marked by collaborations with other artists, revisitations of earlier works, and a deep engagement with contemporary musical trends. He experimented with various genres, blending classical elements with jazz, pop, and world music, showcasing his versatility and openness to new musical frontiers.

Despite facing health challenges and personal losses, including the passing of his beloved wife, Felicia, Bernstein's commitment to music remained steadfast. He continued to conduct, compose, and mentor, leaving an indelible mark on every musician and student he encountered.

In the grand narrative of Leonard Bernstein's life, his final compositions stand as a testament to his enduring genius, passion, and commitment to his craft. They serve as poignant reminders of a maestro who, even in the twilight of his life, continued to inspire, innovate, and touch the hearts of countless individuals through the universal language of music.

27. The Maestro's Reflections: On Life, Love, and Music

Leonard Bernstein, a name synonymous with musical brilliance, was not just a maestro on the podium but also a philosopher at heart. Throughout his life, he grappled with profound questions about art, humanity, love, and the very essence of existence. His reflections, both public and private, provide a window into the soul of a man who lived and breathed music.

Bernstein's musings on life were deeply intertwined with his Jewish heritage. He often spoke about the spiritual connection he felt with music, likening it to a divine language that transcended words. For Bernstein, music was a bridge to the divine, a means to connect with something greater than oneself. This spiritual dimension of his life was evident in many of his works, most notably in his "Kaddish" Symphony, where he wrestled with his relationship with God.

Love, in all its forms, was another recurring theme in Bernstein's reflections. His passionate love for music, his deep affection for his family, and his complex relationships all shaped his understanding of this most universal of emotions. Bernstein believed in the transformative power of love, seeing it as a force that could inspire, heal, and elevate the human spirit.

His relationship with his wife, Felicia Montealegre, was a testament to this belief. Despite the challenges they faced, their bond was one of mutual respect, admiration, and deep affection. Bernstein often spoke of Felicia as his muse, crediting her with inspiring some of his most poignant compositions.

On the topic of music, Bernstein's reflections were vast and varied. He mused about the nature of creativity, the role of the artist in society, and the eternal quest for perfection. He believed that music had the power to communicate universal truths, to bridge divides, and to touch the very core of our being. For Bernstein, every note, every rhythm, every melody was a reflection of life itself.

In various interviews, lectures, and writings, Bernstein shared his thoughts on these topics and more. He spoke candidly about his fears, his hopes, and his dreams. He pondered the challenges of living in a rapidly changing world and the role of the artist in such times. Through all these reflections, one thing remained constant: Bernstein's unwavering belief in the power of music to illuminate, to heal, and to inspire.

As we delve deeper into the life and legacy of Leonard Bernstein, these reflections serve as a guide, shedding light on the mind of a genius and offering insights into the heart of a man who, through his music and his words, sought to make sense of the world around him.

28. A World Without Felicia: Navigating Grief and Legacy

The death of Felicia Montealegre in 1978 was a profound blow to Leonard Bernstein. The two had shared a bond that was as deep as it was complex, and her absence left a void in Bernstein's life that could never truly be filled.

Felicia, an accomplished actress and social activist, had been Bernstein's muse, confidante, and partner in life's journey. Their relationship was marked by mutual respect, admiration, and a shared passion for the arts. While they faced their share of challenges, their love for each other was evident to all who knew them.

After Felicia's passing, Bernstein's behavior began to change. Sources indicate that he became more unpredictable and, at times, outlandish in his actions. The weight of grief, combined with the pressures of his career, took a toll on his mental and emotional well-being. His drug use, which had been a part of his life for years, began to spiral out of control, further exacerbating his emotional turmoil.

Yet, even in his grief, Bernstein's commitment to music and his craft remained unwavering. He continued to compose, conduct, and mentor young musicians, channeling his pain and sorrow into his work. Music became a refuge, a way for him to process his emotions and find solace.

Felicia's influence on Bernstein's life was evident even after her death. He often spoke of her in interviews, recalling their time together with fondness and reverence. Her memory served as a guiding force, inspiring him to push the boundaries of his art and to continue making a difference in the world of music.

In the years following Felicia's death, Bernstein's work took on a more introspective tone. His compositions became more reflective, exploring themes of loss, love, and the passage of time. It was as if he was trying to communicate with Felicia through his music, seeking a connection with her in the only way he knew how.

The loss of Felicia Montealegre was a defining moment in Leonard Bernstein's life. It shaped his later years, influencing his work and his interactions with those around him. Through it all, however, Bernstein's love for Felicia remained a constant, a testament to the enduring power of love and the indelible mark it leaves on our lives.

29. The Final Bow: Bernstein's Last Performances

Leonard Bernstein's illustrious career spanned decades, touching countless lives with his musical genius. As the twilight of his life approached, Bernstein's performances took on a deeper, more profound resonance, reflecting a lifetime of experience, passion, and dedication to his craft.

In the late 1980s and early 1990s, Bernstein's health began to decline, but his commitment to music remained unwavering. He continued to conduct, compose, and mentor, leaving an indelible mark on every stage he graced. Each performance became a testament to his enduring spirit and love for music.

One of the most poignant moments in this phase of his career was his final concert. Bernstein chose to conduct Beethoven's Symphony No. 7, a piece that encapsulates the full range of human emotions, from the exuberant joy of the second movement to the profound depths of the third. This performance, held with the Vienna Philharmonic Orchestra, showcased Bernstein's unparalleled ability to connect with the music and convey its essence to the audience. The maestro's final appearance at Carnegie Hall was on March 11, 1990, conducting this very orchestra, a fitting culmination to a relationship that had spanned decades.

Bernstein's last performances were not just about the music; they were a reflection of his life's journey. They showcased a man who, despite facing the inevitability of time, chose to celebrate life with every note, every gesture, and every moment on stage. These performances were filled with raw emotion, capturing the essence of a man who had given his all to the world of music.

The world watched as Bernstein took his final bows, each one filled with gratitude, humility, and an overwhelming love for music. These moments were bittersweet, marking the end of an era but also celebrating a legacy that would continue to inspire generations to come.

Leonard Bernstein's final performances were a testament to his enduring spirit, his passion for music, and his unwavering commitment to sharing his gift with the world. They serve as a poignant reminder of the power of music to touch our souls, to bring us together, and to leave a lasting impact long after the final note has been played.

30. Legacy in Harmony: The Music and Teachings that Endure

Leonard Bernstein's influence on the musical landscape is profound and enduring. As a conductor, composer, educator, and humanitarian, he touched countless lives, leaving an indelible mark on the world of music.

Bernstein's belief in music's transformative power was evident in every aspect of his career. He viewed music as a universal language, capable of bridging cultural, social, and political divides. This philosophy was brilliantly showcased in his **Young People's Concerts**, televised programs designed to introduce classical music to a younger audience. Through these concerts, Bernstein demystified complex musical concepts, making them accessible and engaging for all.

Beyond these concerts, Bernstein's commitment to education was unwavering. Often described as an "incessant teacher," he seized every opportunity to impart knowledge, whether through formal lectures at prestigious institutions or spontaneous lessons during rehearsals. He believed in the potential of every individual to connect with and appreciate music, regardless of their background.

But Bernstein's teachings extended beyond the notes and rhythms. He encouraged listeners to delve deeper, to explore the philosophical and societal contexts of compositions. He challenged conventions and prompted critical thinking, pushing boundaries in both music and thought.

Various institutions and resources, such as the **Leonard Bernstein Office**, continue to uphold and promote his educational ideals. They serve as a testament to the cyclical nature of teaching and learning, emphasizing the profound impact of mentors and teachers.

Leonard Bernstein's legacy is multifaceted. It's a blend of musical brilliance, educational prowess, and a deep-seated passion for sharing the joy of music. Through his contributions, he has ensured that his spirit and teachings will resonate with future generations, inspiring them to explore the boundless world of music.

31. The Maestro's Students: Protégés and Successors

Leonard Bernstein's influence extended far beyond his own compositions and performances. As a dedicated educator and mentor, he nurtured the talents of many young musicians, ensuring that his legacy would continue through their work.

Throughout his career, Bernstein was known for his hands-on approach to teaching. He believed in the power of experiential learning, often inviting young musicians to join him in rehearsals or even on stage. This provided them with invaluable real-world experience and a unique insight into the maestro's methods and mindset.

Many of Bernstein's protégés went on to have successful careers of their own, carrying forward the lessons they learned under his tutelage. Some became renowned conductors, while others excelled as composers, performers, or educators. Yet, regardless of their chosen path, the influence of their time with Bernstein was evident in their work.

One notable protégé was **Michael Tilson Thomas**, who has often spoken about the profound impact Bernstein had on his career. Thomas recalls the invaluable lessons he learned from the maestro, both in terms of technical skills and the deeper philosophical approach to music.

Another significant figure influenced by Bernstein was Marin Alsop, a trailblazing female conductor who often cites Bernstein as a key mentor in her journey. Alsop's dynamic and passionate approach to conducting reflects the teachings and spirit of Bernstein.

Beyond these individual success stories, Bernstein's influence can be seen in the broader world of music education. His methods, teachings, and philosophies have been integrated into curricula worldwide, ensuring that future generations of musicians benefit from his wisdom.

In the world of classical music, the role of a mentor is paramount. The knowledge, skills, and insights passed down from one generation to the next ensure the continued growth and evolution of the art form. And in this grand tapestry of musical mentorship, Leonard Bernstein's legacy stands out as particularly influential. Through his protégés and successors, his teachings and passion for music continue to resonate, shaping the future of classical music.

32. Felicia's Echo: Remembering Her Impact

Felicia Montealegre Bernstein, born Felicia María Cohn Montealegre on February 6, 1922, was much more than just the wife of the renowned maestro Leonard Bernstein. She was a force in her own right, a Costa Rican-Chilean actress who left an indelible mark on the world of arts, both on and off the stage.

Felicia's career blossomed during the Golden Age of Television. She was known for her **major television network appearances** and roles in theaters, opera houses, and concert halls worldwide. Her performances in televised dramas and theatrical roles, both on and off Broadway, garnered her significant acclaim.

But beyond her professional achievements, Felicia was a beacon of strength and grace in her personal life. Her marriage to Leonard Bernstein was filled with love, challenges, and mutual respect. The couple faced their share of trials, particularly given Leonard's infidelity, but their bond remained strong. Felicia's resilience and unwavering support for her husband, even during the most challenging times, showcased her character's depth.

Felicia's letters, which have been referenced in various biographies and articles, provide a window into her soul. They reveal a woman of profound depth, intelligence, and sensitivity. These letters, exchanged with Leonard and other close confidants, offer insights into her thoughts, feelings, and the intricacies of her relationship with the maestro.

One poignant quote from a letter to Leonard reads, "Our love is so deep and profound that it has its own life. It breathes, it speaks, it sings, it cries. It is the essence of who we are, and it will endure, even when we are no more."

Felicia's impact extended beyond her family. She was an active social activist, using her platform to champion various causes and make a difference in the world. Her commitment to social justice and her passion for the arts made her a beloved figure in many circles.

Tragically, Felicia's life was cut short when she passed away from lung cancer in East Hampton, New York, on June 16, 1978, at the age of 56. Her loss was deeply felt by Leonard, their children, and the broader artistic community.

Today, Felicia Montealegre Bernstein's legacy lives on. Through her performances, her activism, and her enduring love story with Leonard Bernstein, she remains an inspiration to many. Her life serves as a testament to the power of love, resilience, and the indomitable human spirit.

33. The Maestro's Awards: Celebrating a Life of Achievement

Leonard Bernstein's illustrious career was marked not only by his immense talent and contributions to music but also by the numerous accolades he received in recognition of his work. These awards serve as a testament to his enduring impact on the world of music and beyond.

Throughout his lifetime, Bernstein was honored with a staggering **16 Grammy Awards**, including one for Lifetime Achievement. These Grammys spanned various categories, recognizing both his conducting prowess and his compositions. His work on "Candide" with the London Symphony Orchestra & Chorus, for instance, earned him the **1991 Grammy Award for Best Classical Album**.

In addition to his Grammy triumphs, Bernstein was the recipient of **seven Emmy Awards**. These Emmys celebrated his efforts in bringing classical music to television audiences, further cementing his reputation as a pioneer in making classical music accessible to the masses.

Bernstein's achievements weren't limited to music alone. He was also honored with **two Tony Awards** for his contributions to Broadway, showcasing his versatility as a musician and composer.

Beyond these major awards, Bernstein was bestowed with numerous other honors. He received Honorary Degrees from esteemed institutions like **Northwestern University** and Hebrew Union College. Foreign governments also recognized his contributions, and he was decorated with various international awards.

In 1981, Bernstein's contributions to the arts were further acknowledged when he received the prestigious **Kennedy Center Honor**. This award, given to individuals who have enriched American culture through the performing arts, was a fitting tribute to a man who had dedicated his life to music and education.

While awards and accolades are a tangible recognition of an artist's contributions, Leonard Bernstein's true legacy lies in the music he created, the lives he touched, and the countless musicians and audiences he inspired. These awards, while significant, are but a small reflection of the profound impact he had on the world of music and the arts.

34. Felicia's Charities: Her Commitment to Philanthropy

Felicia Montealegre Bernstein was not just a talented actress and the wife of the legendary Leonard Bernstein; she was also a dedicated philanthropist and social justice activist. Her commitment to making a difference in the world was evident in the numerous causes she championed and the organizations she supported.

Felicia was deeply involved with the **American Civil Liberties Union**, where she chaired the Women's Division. Her dedication to civil liberties and human rights was unwavering, and she worked tirelessly to ensure that these fundamental rights were protected for all.

In addition to her work with the ACLU, Felicia co-founded **"Another Mother for Peace"**, an antiwar organization that aimed to promote peace and end the violence of war. This organization was a testament to her belief in the power of collective action and the importance of advocating for a more peaceful world.

One of the most notable events that highlighted Felicia's commitment to social justice was her involvement in hosting a controversial fundraiser to support the families of the **"Black Panther 21"**. This event showcased her willingness to take a stand for what she believed in, even when faced with criticism and backlash.

Felicia's activism was not limited to just these organizations. She was also arrested at an **antiwar protest in Washington, DC**, further showcasing her dedication to the causes she believed in.

To honor Felicia's memory and continue their joint struggle for human rights, Leonard Bernstein established the **Felicia Montealegre Bernstein Fund of Amnesty International USA**. This fund was the first of its kind in Amnesty and aimed to provide support for human rights activists who had limited resources but immense dedication to the cause.

Felicia Montealegre Bernstein's legacy as a philanthropist and activist is a testament to her deep commitment to making the world a better place. Through her tireless efforts and unwavering dedication, she left an indelible mark on the causes she championed and the lives she touched.

35. The Maestro's Recordings: A Life in Albums

Leonard Bernstein's discography is a rich tapestry that encapsulates his profound dedication to music. Each recording, be it of a revered classical piece, a Broadway hit, or a modern composition, offers a glimpse into his evolving journey as a conductor, composer, and pianist.

With the New York Philharmonic, Bernstein breathed new life into classical compositions, making them resonate with both seasoned aficionados and newcomers to the genre. His interpretations were characterized by their vitality, depth, and personal touch, revealing a deep, emotional connection to every note he conducted.

His original compositions, such as the iconic scores for "West Side Story" and "Candide," stand as monuments to his creative genius. Through these recordings, one can trace the maturation of his musical style, discern the myriad influences that molded him, and appreciate the pioneering techniques he embraced.

Collaborations with international orchestras showcased Bernstein's global reach and his knack for bridging cultural divides. These partnerships underscored his adaptability, his reverence for diverse musical traditions, and his vision of a world united by the universal language of music.

But Bernstein's recordings are more than mere musical tracks. They serve as historical markers, echoing the evolving musical zeitgeist of the 20th century, chronicling the peaks and valleys of his illustrious career, and bearing witness to the indelible mark he left on the musical world.

Leonard Bernstein's albums are not just auditory experiences; they are narratives. They tell the story of a maestro's life, his passions, his challenges, and the timeless legacy he bequeathed to the world of music.

36. Felicia's Art: Exploring Her Lesser-Known Talents

Felicia Montealegre Bernstein, often overshadowed by her husband's towering musical legacy, was a force of nature in her own right. Born Felicia María Cohn Montealegre, she hailed from a Costa Rican-Chilean background and carved a niche for herself in the world of arts, both on and off the stage.

Felicia's talents were multifaceted. She was a renowned actress, celebrated for her performances in televised dramas during the dawn of the Golden Age of Television. Her roles spanned major television networks, theaters on Broadway and beyond, opera houses, and concert halls across the globe. Her ability to captivate audiences with her powerful performances was a testament to her dedication and passion for the craft.

Beyond her acting prowess, Felicia was also an accomplished pianist and singer. Her musical inclinations were evident in her ability to seamlessly blend into the world of classical music, often accompanying her husband in various performances and events. This shared love for music undoubtedly played a pivotal role in their relationship, creating a harmonious bond that transcended the usual dynamics of marital life.

But perhaps one of the lesser-known facets of Felicia's artistic journey was her foray into the visual arts. She was an amateur painter and sculptor, often using these mediums to express her innermost thoughts and emotions. While her artworks might not have gained the same level of recognition as her performances, they provided a window into her soul, revealing a side of her that was introspective, sensitive, and deeply connected to the world around her.

Felicia's commitment to philanthropy was another testament to her multifaceted personality. She was deeply involved in various charitable endeavors, using her platform to advocate for causes close to her heart. Her dedication to making a difference, both through her art and her philanthropic efforts, showcased a woman who was not just content with being in the spotlight but was driven by a desire to impact the world positively.

In delving into Felicia Montealegre Bernstein's life, one discovers a woman of immense talent, depth, and compassion. Her contributions to the arts, her unwavering support for her husband's endeavors, and her commitment to making a difference paint a portrait of a woman who, in many ways, was ahead of her time. Through her art, her music, and her philanthropy, Felicia left an indelible mark on the world, ensuring that her legacy would endure for generations to come.

37. The Maestro's Words: Interviews, Speeches, and Writings

Leonard Bernstein's voice echoed not just through his compositions but also through the myriad of interviews, speeches, and writings he left behind. Each word, each phrase, was a testament to his profound understanding of music, life, and the intricate dance between the two.

One could feel the depth of his passion when he remarked, "Music can name the unnameable and communicate the unknowable." It wasn't just a statement; it was a belief, a philosophy that Bernstein lived by. Music, for him, was a language beyond words, capable of expressing the deepest human emotions and experiences.

His commitment to the essence of music was evident when he said, "I'm not interested in having an orchestra sound like itself. I want it to sound like the composer." Bernstein wasn't just conducting pieces; he was breathing life into the composer's vision, ensuring that every note played was a true reflection of its creator's intent.

But Bernstein's eloquence wasn't confined to music alone. He had a unique way of looking at the world, often with a touch of humor. "I've been all over the world and I've never seen a statue of a critic," he quipped once, highlighting the transient nature of criticism against the enduring legacy of creativity.

In moments of introspection, he would often delve deep into the philosophy of life. "Stillness is our most intense mode of action," he mused, emphasizing the importance of reflection and inner peace in a world constantly in motion.

And then there were times when he would offer insights laced with humor, such as when he observed, "To achieve great things, two things are needed: a plan and not quite enough time." It was a nod to the unpredictable nature of creativity, where constraints often lead to the most profound innovations.

Through all these words and many more, Leonard Bernstein continues to inspire, challenge, and enlighten generations of music lovers and thinkers. His legacy is not just in the notes he composed but also in the wisdom he shared.

38. Felicia's Wisdom: Quotes and Reflections

Felicia Montealegre Bernstein, a talented actress and the wife of Leonard Bernstein, was a woman of depth and insight. Her life, intertwined with that of the Maestro, was filled with moments of joy, challenges, and profound reflections. Through her letters, interviews, and personal writings, Felicia's voice emerges, offering a unique perspective on life, love, and art.

One of the most poignant letters she wrote to Leonard was a testament to her understanding and acceptance of him. She wrote, "Third: I am willing to accept you as you are, without being a martyr or sacrificing myself on the L.B. altar. (I happen to love you very much - this may be a disease and if it is what better...". This letter, among others, showcased her deep love for Leonard, acknowledging his complexities and embracing them.

Felicia's wisdom wasn't just confined to her relationship with Leonard. As an actress, she had her own insights into the world of art and performance. She once remarked about the ephemeral nature of acting, suggesting that while the performance might be transient, the impact it leaves on the audience is everlasting.

Her commitment to philanthropy and social causes also reflected her deep sense of responsibility to the world around her. Felicia believed in using her platform to make a difference, to bring about positive change, and to uplift those less fortunate.

In her interactions with friends and family, Felicia often shared pearls of wisdom, reflecting on the nature of life, relationships, and the human experience. Her words, filled with empathy and understanding, served as a guiding light for many who knew her.

Felicia's reflections, combined with her experiences, paint a picture of a woman who was not just the wife of a famous composer but a force to be reckoned with in her own right. Her wisdom, gleaned from a life rich in experiences, continues to inspire and resonate with those who delve into her writings and memories.

39. The Maestro's Mentors: Those Who Guided Bernstein

In the world of music, mentors play an indispensable role in shaping the careers and artistic visions of budding talents. Leonard Bernstein, despite his innate genius, was no exception. Throughout his life, he was fortunate to be guided by several luminaries in the music world, each of whom left an indelible mark on his journey.

One of the most influential figures in Bernstein's early career was **Fritz Reiner**. As a student at the Curtis Institute, Bernstein had the opportunity to study conducting under Reiner's tutelage. Reiner's meticulous attention to detail and his profound understanding of orchestral nuances provided Bernstein with a solid foundation in the art of conducting.

Another pivotal mentor in Bernstein's life was **Aaron Copland**. Not only did Copland play a significant role in Bernstein's musical education, but he also became a lifelong friend. Copland's encouragement was instrumental in Bernstein introducing himself to **Serge Koussevitzky**, the then conductor of the Boston

Symphony Orchestra. Koussevitzky recognized Bernstein's potential early on and became a guiding force, helping him navigate the complexities of the music world.

The relationship between Bernstein and Koussevitzky was profound. Koussevitzky's belief in Bernstein's talent and his unwavering support played a crucial role in Bernstein's rise to prominence. Under Koussevitzky's mentorship, Bernstein honed his skills, developing a unique style that combined passion with precision.

Apart from these stalwarts, Bernstein was also influenced by other prominent figures in the music world, such as **Dmitri Mitropoulos**. Bernstein's encounter with Mitropoulos's passionate performance left a lasting impression on him, further fueling his desire to excel in the realm of conducting.

These mentors, with their vast reservoirs of knowledge and experience, provided Bernstein with the tools, guidance, and confidence he needed to carve out his path. Their teachings, combined with Bernstein's innate talent, culminated in the creation of a maestro whose legacy continues to inspire generations of musicians.

40. Felicia's Circle: Friends and Influences

Felicia Montealegre Bernstein, a stunningly beautiful Chilean stage and television actress, had a life that was as vibrant and multifaceted as her husband's. Beyond her marriage to Leonard Bernstein, Felicia carved out her own niche in the world of arts, making significant contributions and forming lasting relationships with many prominent figures.

Felicia's career blossomed during the Golden Age of Television. She was known for her major television network appearances, including roles in *Goodyear Theatre* and *The Kaiser Aluminum Hour*. Her portrayal of Empress Carlotta Amelia in *Goodyear Theatre* and Ismene in *The Kaiser Aluminum Hour* were particularly noteworthy.

One of her most cherished professional relationships was with the renowned director Mike Nichols. Felicia returned to the Broadway stage in 1967 to play Birdie Hubbard in Lillian Hellman's *The Little Foxes*, directed by Nichols. This collaboration showcased her versatility as an actress and further solidified her reputation in the theater world.

Felicia's influence wasn't limited to the stage. She was also an active social activist, using her platform to advocate for causes close to her heart. Her commitment to philanthropy and social justice mirrored that of her husband, making them a formidable pair in both the arts and activism.

Her personal circle was a blend of artists, activists, and intellectuals. Among her close friends and acquaintances were individuals from various fields, each contributing to the rich tapestry of her life. These relationships provided Felicia with a diverse range of perspectives, enriching her own worldview and influencing her artistic choices.

One of the most touching aspects of Felicia's life was her correspondence. Letters exchanged between her and Leonard provide a deeply personal insight into their relationship, revealing the depth of their love, the challenges they faced, and the mutual respect they held for each other. These letters, some of which have been made public, offer a window into Felicia's soul, showcasing her eloquence, wisdom, and unwavering love for her family.

In essence, Felicia Montealegre Bernstein was not just the wife of a maestro; she was a force to be reckoned with in her own right. Her legacy, both as an artist and as a compassionate human being, continues to inspire and resonate with many, even decades after her passing.

41. The Maestro's Opera: Diving into New Musical Realms

Leonard Bernstein, renowned for his versatility, ventured into the world of opera, adding another dimension to his already illustrious career. His foray into this genre showcased his ability to weave intricate narratives with compelling music, creating masterpieces that resonated with audiences and critics alike.

One of Bernstein's most notable contributions to the opera world is "Trouble in Tahiti," a one-act opera he wrote in 1952. Set in post-war suburban America, it delves into the disillusionment of a young couple, Sam and Dinah, as they grapple with the realities of their seemingly perfect life. The opera, with its jazz-infused score and poignant narrative, offers a critique of the American dream and the pursuit of happiness.

A more complex and layered work came later in the form of "A Quiet Place." Premiered in 1983, this opera serves as both a sequel to "Trouble in Tahiti" and a standalone piece. It explores the dynamics of the same family, years after the events of the first opera, as they come to terms with grief, acceptance, and reconciliation. The music, rich and varied, draws from various genres, reflecting the multifaceted emotions of the characters.

Bernstein's collaboration with choreographer Jerome Robbins also led to the creation of major ballets like "Fancy Free" (1944) and "Dybbuk" (1975). While not operas in the traditional sense, these ballets showcased Bernstein's ability to craft compelling narratives through music and dance.

Furthermore, his operetta "Candide," based on Voltaire's novella, is a testament to Bernstein's ability to merge the worlds of Broadway and opera. With its satirical narrative and eclectic score, "Candide" has become a staple in both the opera and musical theater repertoires.

Bernstein's ventures into the realm of opera and ballet underscore his ceaseless quest for innovation and his ability to transcend musical boundaries. Through these works, he not only enriched the operatic repertoire but also showcased the universality of musical storytelling.

42. Felicia's Resilience: Facing Illness with Grace

Felicia Montealegre Bernstein, a woman of immense talent and grace, faced one of life's most formidable challenges with a resilience that left an indelible mark on those around her. Diagnosed with lung cancer, Felicia's journey through illness was a testament to her strength, spirit, and unwavering love for her family.

Born in Costa Rica and raised in Chile, Felicia Montealegre was not just Leonard Bernstein's wife but also an accomplished actress. Her career spanned major television network appearances, roles in theaters on and off Broadway, opera houses, and concert halls worldwide. As her career blossomed during the Golden Age of Television, so did her reputation as a formidable talent.

However, beyond the spotlight, Felicia was a pillar of strength for her family. When diagnosed with lung cancer, she faced the illness with a grace that was both inspiring and heart-wrenching. Throughout her battle, Felicia remained positive, drawing strength from her love for Leonard and their children. Her resilience in the face of adversity was a testament to her character and the depth of her spirit.

In letters and personal reflections, Felicia often spoke of the importance of love, family, and the arts in her life. Even in her most challenging moments, she found solace in music, theater, and the arts, which had always been her passion. Her relationship with Leonard was a source of immense strength, and their bond only deepened during her illness.

Felicia Montealegre Bernstein passed away in East Hampton, New York, on June 16, 1978, at the age of 56. Her departure left a void in the world of arts and in the hearts of those who knew and loved her. Yet, her legacy endures, not just through her contributions to the arts but also through the lessons of resilience, grace, and love she imparted during her lifetime.

In the end, Felicia's life story is a testament to the power of the human spirit to overcome adversity, the importance of love and family, and the enduring impact of art on the soul. Her journey, marked by both triumphs and challenges, serves as an inspiration to all who face life's trials with courage, grace, and an unwavering spirit.

43. The Maestro's Inspirations: What Drove Bernstein's Genius

Leonard Bernstein's genius was not an isolated spark but a flame fueled by a myriad of inspirations. Born into a Jewish family, the rich traditions, stories, and melodies from his heritage deeply influenced his musical sensibilities. This cultural backdrop provided a foundation upon which he built his vast repertoire.

As he ventured into the world of music, Bernstein was fortunate to be under the tutelage of some of the best in the business. His early years with the New York Philharmonic, especially the pivotal moment when he substituted for conductor Bruno Walter in 1943, were not just about showcasing his talent but also about absorbing the wisdom of those around him.

His compositions often mirrored his life. The "Symphony No. 2: The Age of Anxiety," inspired by W.H. Auden's poem, is a testament to Bernstein's ability to translate literary works into musical masterpieces. It reflected the societal angst of the times, showcasing his knack for capturing the zeitgeist in his melodies.

Broadway and Hollywood also beckoned Bernstein. His scores, such as the one for 1954's "On the Waterfront," showcased his versatility. These compositions were not just about creating music but about blending classical ethos with contemporary themes.

But perhaps, one of the most profound influences on his music was his personal life. His relationship with his wife, Felicia Montealegre, was a roller-coaster of emotions. The love, the pain, the highs, and the lows with Felicia found echoes in his compositions, making them deeply personal yet universally relatable.

Bernstein's commitment to education was another driving force. He believed in the power of music education and worked tirelessly to demystify classical music, making it accessible to all. His television programs, lectures, and writings were not just about teaching but about sharing his passion with the world.

The changing political and social landscape of the 1960s and 70s also left its mark on Bernstein. His music from this era resonated with the times, reflecting his activism and his stance on issues like the Civil Rights Movement and the Vietnam War.

In the vast expanse of Leonard Bernstein's life, each experience, each interaction, and each inspiration added depth and dimension. His genius was a harmonious blend of his experiences, his interactions, and his innate talent, marking him as a truly exceptional musician.

44. Felicia's Footprints: Her Lasting Mark on the Arts

Felicia Montealegre Bernstein, often overshadowed by the towering legacy of her husband, Leonard Bernstein, was a force to be reckoned with in her own right. Born in Costa Rica and later moving to Chile, Felicia's early life was marked by a rich cultural tapestry that would influence her artistic pursuits.

Upon her arrival in New York City, Felicia began her acting lessons with Herbert Berghof at the Dramatic Workshop of the New School for Social Research. She continued her studies with him at his newly-founded acting school, HB Studio. Her dedication and talent soon saw her making significant strides in the world of theater, both on and off Broadway.

Felicia's career blossomed during the Golden Age of Television. She made appearances in major television network shows, including "Kraft Television Theatre," "Suspense," "Studio One," and "The Chevrolet Tele-Theatre." Her versatility as an actor was evident as she seamlessly transitioned between different roles, captivating audiences with her performances.

Beyond her acting career, Felicia was also a social activist. She used her platform to advocate for causes close to her heart, ensuring that her voice was heard in spheres beyond the arts. Her commitment to philanthropy and social causes showcased a side of her that was deeply empathetic and driven to make a difference.

Felicia's personal life, especially her relationship with Leonard Bernstein, was filled with complexities. Their correspondence, filled with love, passion, understanding, and at times, pain, offers a deep insight into their bond. One particularly poignant letter from Felicia to Leonard highlights the challenges they faced due to his sexuality. Despite the hurdles, their love for each other remained steadfast, with Felicia often being Leonard's anchor during tumultuous times.

In the world of arts, Felicia Montealegre Bernstein left an indelible mark. Whether it was through her performances, her activism, or her role as a muse for one of the greatest composers of the 20th century, Felicia's legacy is a testament to her talent, resilience, and unwavering spirit.

45. The Maestro's Challenges: Personal Struggles in the Spotlight

Leonard Bernstein, a name synonymous with musical genius, was not just a maestro on the podium but also a complex individual off it. His life, both personal and professional, was a series of highs and lows, triumphs and challenges.

Bernstein's rise to fame was meteoric, but with that fame came intense scrutiny. The public's fascination with his life was insatiable. Every performance, every appearance, and every statement he made was dissected and discussed. The pressure to constantly be at his best, both as a conductor and as a composer, was immense.

One of the most significant personal challenges Bernstein faced was reconciling his sexuality. Living in a time when being openly gay was not only socially unacceptable but also professionally risky, Bernstein often found himself torn between his true self and the image he presented to the world. Articles like the one titled **"Inside Leonard Bernstein's 'slow creep toward overt gayness'"** shed light on his struggles with his sexuality and the impact it had on his personal and professional relationships.

Bernstein's relationship with his wife, Felicia Montealegre, was another area of his life that was under constant scrutiny. Their bond was deep, filled with love, understanding, and at times, pain. Felicia was aware of Bernstein's sexuality, and their correspondence, filled with passion and understanding, offers a deep insight into their complex relationship.

Beyond his personal life, Bernstein faced challenges in his professional life as well. His political beliefs and activism, especially during the tumultuous 1960s, often put him at odds with conservative elements in society. His association with various social and political causes, while commendable, also made him a target for criticism.

Yet, despite the challenges and controversies, Bernstein's legacy as a musician remains untarnished. His contributions to the world of classical music, his innovative approach to teaching, and his ability to bridge the gap between classical and popular music ensure that he will always be remembered as one of the greatest musical minds of the 20th century.

46. Felicia's Voice: Her Role in Bernstein's Life

Felicia Montealegre, a captivating figure in her own right, played an instrumental role in Leonard Bernstein's life. Born in San José, Costa Rica, on February 6, 1922, Felicia was a woman of many talents, including acting and music. Her mother, Clemencia Montealegre of Costa Rica, belonged to a large family, with Felicia being the second daughter. Felicia's early life saw her establishing herself in New York, where she even took piano lessons from the renowned Chilean pianist Claudio Arrau.

Felicia and Leonard's paths first crossed at a party in 1946. Their connection was immediate, and the two quickly fell in love. By 1951, they were married, marking the beginning of a partnership that would endure personal and professional challenges. Felicia was not just Bernstein's wife but also his muse, confidante, and most significant supporter. Their relationship was deep, filled with mutual respect, understanding, and love.

Throughout their marriage, Felicia was a grounding force for Bernstein. She provided stability in the whirlwind of his fame and was often the voice of reason during his moments of doubt. Their correspondence, filled with passion, understanding, and sometimes pain, offers a profound insight into their complex relationship. Felicia was well aware of Bernstein's struggles with his sexuality, and their letters reveal a bond that transcended societal norms and expectations.

In addition to her role as Bernstein's partner, Felicia was an accomplished artist in her own right. She had a successful acting career, debuting on Broadway in Ben Hecht and Charles MacArthur's "Swan Song." Her concert performances also included several collaborations with her husband, showcasing her musical talents.

However, Felicia's impact on Bernstein's life wasn't limited to their personal relationship. She played a pivotal role in his professional journey, often offering insights, feedback, and encouragement. Her influence can be seen in many of Bernstein's works, where her presence and essence are palpable.

Tragically, Felicia's life was cut short by illness, but her legacy lives on. Through her art, her philanthropic endeavors, and most importantly, her profound influence on one of the 20th century's greatest musical minds, Felicia Montealegre remains an indelible figure in the annals of music history.

47. The Maestro's Humanitarian Efforts: Music for a Cause

Leonard Bernstein was not just a musical genius; he was also a man deeply committed to social justice and humanitarian causes. Throughout his life, he used his platform and influence to advocate for change, believing in the power of music to heal, unite, and inspire.

In the tumultuous 1960s, Bernstein became an outspoken advocate for civil rights. He participated in benefit concerts to raise funds for organizations like the Congress of Racial Equality (CORE) and the Student Nonviolent Coordinating Committee (SNCC). His commitment to racial equality was unwavering, and he often collaborated with other artists and activists to amplify the message of justice and equality.

Beyond the civil rights movement, Bernstein was also deeply concerned about global issues. He was a vocal critic of the Vietnam War and used his music to protest against it. In 1973, he conducted a peace concert in Washington, D.C., where he performed with the National

Symphony Orchestra, sending a powerful message of peace and unity.

Bernstein's humanitarian spirit extended to issues of poverty and education as well. He believed in the transformative power of music education and was instrumental in creating programs to bring music to underprivileged communities. One such initiative was the "El Sistema" program in Venezuela, which aimed to provide free musical education to children in impoverished areas. This program has since become a global phenomenon, changing the lives of countless young musicians.

In the later years of his life, Bernstein turned his attention to the AIDS crisis, which was ravaging the artistic community. He organized and performed in numerous benefit concerts to raise funds for AIDS research and to support those affected by the disease.

Leonard Bernstein's humanitarian efforts were a testament to his belief in the power of music to effect change. He once said, "This will be our reply to violence: to make music more intensely, more beautifully, more devotedly than ever before." And throughout his life, he did just that, using his art to advocate for a better, more just world.

48. Felicia's Foundations: Building a Legacy of Giving

Felicia Montealegre Bernstein was not just an artist; she was a beacon of compassion and philanthropy. Her Costa Rican-Chilean heritage, combined with her experiences in the arts, shaped her worldview and her commitment to making a tangible difference.

Felicia's artistic journey took her through the Golden Age of Television, where she graced screens and stages, both on and off Broadway. She collaborated with symphony orchestras across the United States, often sharing the stage with her husband, Leonard Bernstein, in dramatic and narrating roles.

Yet, away from the limelight, Felicia's heart was deeply rooted in charitable endeavors. She believed that art and culture had the power to catalyze positive societal change. This belief drove her to support various causes, leveraging her platform to amplify awareness and gather resources.

One of her most impactful contributions was to human rights. Recognizing her unwavering commitment, Leonard Bernstein inaugurated the **Felicia Montealegre Bernstein Fund of Amnesty International USA**. This initiative was designed to bolster human rights activists with limited means, marking a pioneering step for Amnesty International and reflecting the couple's shared dedication to human rights advocacy.

Beyond human rights, Felicia's charitable spirit found expression in numerous other avenues. She often operated away from the public eye, silently driving change. Today, her legacy of benevolence serves as a beacon, exemplifying the profound impact an individual can have.

Felicia Montealegre Bernstein's enduring legacy is a testament to her conviction in the transformative potential of art, culture, and philanthropy. Through her endeavors and the institutions she championed, she has sown seeds of compassion and change that continue to flourish.

49. The Maestro's Vision: Bernstein's Hopes for the Future

Leonard Bernstein, throughout his illustrious career, was not just a musician but also a visionary. His beliefs, aspirations, and dreams for the future of music and society at large were deeply intertwined with his personal experiences and the evolving world around him.

Bernstein's vision for the future of music was rooted in his unwavering belief in its universal power. He saw music as a bridge, a tool that could connect diverse cultures, ideologies, and generations. This belief was evident in his numerous educational endeavors, from his Young People's Concerts with the New York Philharmonic to his Harvard lectures. He hoped to democratize classical music, making it accessible and relevant to all, regardless of background or education.

Beyond the realm of music, Bernstein held profound hopes for a more just and peaceful world. Living through some of the most tumultuous times in modern history, including World War II, the Cold War, and the Civil Rights Movement, he witnessed firsthand the devastating impact of division and conflict. Yet, he remained optimistic, believing in humanity's capacity for change and growth. He often spoke of a future where art, education, and mutual respect would pave the way for global harmony.

His commitment to social justice and peace was not just theoretical. Bernstein actively participated in various movements, using his platform to advocate for change. Whether it was performing at peace concerts, supporting civil rights initiatives, or speaking out against war and violence, he consistently aligned his actions with his vision for a better future.

Bernstein's hopes for the future also extended to his personal life. As a father, he wished for a world where his children could thrive, free from prejudice and filled with opportunities. He instilled in them a love for music, culture, and humanity, hoping they would carry forward his legacy of compassion and understanding.

In the end, Leonard Bernstein's vision for the future was a reflection of his life's work and values. He dreamt of a world united by music, understanding, and love—a world where the barriers that divide us would crumble, replaced by bridges of harmony and collaboration.

50. Felicia's Dreams: Her Aspirations and Desires

Felicia Montealegre Bernstein, with her multifaceted personality, held aspirations that spanned both the personal and the universal. Her dreams were deeply rooted in her experiences, her passions, and her vision for the world around her.

From her early days, Felicia's love for performance was evident. She didn't just seek roles; she yearned for characters that allowed her to delve deep into the human psyche, to portray the myriad emotions and relationships that define our existence. Every role was an opportunity to connect, to communicate, and to touch the audience's soul.

As a mother, her aspirations were centered around her children. She envisioned a nurturing environment where they could freely explore their passions, learn the importance of empathy, and grow into individuals who value art and culture as tools for understanding. She hoped they would carry forward the legacy of love for the arts, using it as a bridge to connect with diverse perspectives.

On a broader scale, Felicia dreamt of a world where art played a pivotal role in fostering unity. In a time of significant cultural shifts, she believed that art could transcend boundaries, creating dialogues and building bridges of understanding. This vision wasn't just theoretical; it was reflected in her active support for causes close to her heart, from human rights to arts education.

Her personal relationships also held a special place in her dreams. Felicia valued deep connections, and she aspired to be a beacon of support and love for her friends and family. Her letters, filled with insights and reflections, showcase a woman who cherished every bond and sought to nurture them with genuine affection and understanding.

Felicia Montealegre Bernstein's aspirations paint a picture of a woman deeply in tune with herself and the world around her. Through her life's journey, she strived to realize these dreams, leaving behind a legacy of love, art, and compassion.

51. The Maestro's Innovations: Pioneering New Sounds

Leonard Bernstein's name is synonymous with musical innovation. Throughout his career, he consistently pushed the boundaries of classical music, introducing fresh sounds, techniques, and interpretations that would leave an indelible mark on the world of music.

From his early days as a conductor and composer, Bernstein displayed an innate ability to blend various musical genres seamlessly. His compositions often drew inspiration from jazz, blues, and even rock and roll, creating a unique fusion that resonated with both classical aficionados and the general public. This ability to bridge the gap between the traditional and the contemporary was one of his defining traits.

One of Bernstein's most notable innovations was his approach to rhythm. He believed that rhythm was the lifeblood of music, and he often experimented with unconventional time signatures and syncopations. This rhythmic exploration added a dynamic quality to his compositions, making them feel alive and pulsating with energy.

His work on Broadway, especially "West Side Story," showcased his innovative spirit. Here, Bernstein melded classical techniques with modern musical theater elements, creating a soundscape that was both familiar and groundbreaking. The score, with its intricate orchestrations and daring harmonies, redefined what was possible in musical theater.

Bernstein's innovations weren't limited to composition. As a conductor, he introduced new techniques and interpretations that challenged traditional norms. He believed in the power of emotion in music and often encouraged his orchestras to play with passion and intensity. This emotional connection transformed the listening experience, making each performance a deeply personal journey for the audience.

His collaborations with other artists and musicians further expanded his innovative reach. By working with poets, playwrights, and choreographers, Bernstein explored new ways to tell stories through music, often blurring the lines between different art forms.

In his later years, Bernstein continued to innovate, delving into lesser-known works and championing contemporary composers. He believed that music was an ever-evolving art form, and he dedicated his life to ensuring that it continued to grow, change, and inspire.

Leonard Bernstein's legacy of innovation is a testament to his genius and his unwavering belief in the transformative power of music. Through his pioneering sounds and techniques, he opened new horizons for musicians and listeners alike, forever changing the landscape of classical music.

52: Felicia's Memories: Recollections from Friends and Family

Felicia Montealegre Bernstein, while often recognized as the wife of the legendary Leonard Bernstein, was a luminous figure in her own right. Her impact on those around her was profound, and the memories shared by friends and family offer a deeply personal glimpse into her life, character, and spirit.

Friends often spoke of Felicia's warmth and generosity. She had an innate ability to make those around her feel seen and valued. Her home was a haven for many, a place where artists, musicians, and intellectuals gathered for stimulating conversations and heartfelt connections. Many recall the laughter-filled evenings, where Felicia played the gracious hostess, ensuring everyone felt at ease.

Her close friend, actress Katharine Hepburn, once remarked on Felicia's magnetic presence. "She had this aura," Hepburn noted, "a blend of elegance and genuine kindness. Being around Felicia was like basking in a gentle sun."

Felicia's children, Jamie, Alexander, and Nina, have shared touching anecdotes about their mother. They remember her as a pillar of strength, always there to offer guidance, love, and support. Jamie, in particular, spoke of the bedtime stories Felicia would craft, weaving tales filled with adventure, love, and lessons on kindness.

Nina recalled the afternoons spent with her mother, exploring art galleries and attending theater rehearsals. "She introduced me to the world of art," Nina said, "and taught me to appreciate beauty in all its forms."

Alexander reminisced about the quiet moments, the times when it was just him and his mother, sharing stories and dreams. "She had this ability to listen," he said, "to really listen. And in those moments, I felt truly understood."

Colleagues from the world of theater and arts often spoke of Felicia's dedication and passion. Her performances were lauded not just for her technical prowess but for the emotion she brought to each role. Playwright Tennessee

Williams, who worked with Felicia on several projects, once commented, "Felicia doesn't just act. She lives the character, and that's what makes her performances so memorable."

These memories, shared by those who knew Felicia intimately, paint a portrait of a woman who lived with grace, passion, and an unwavering commitment to her loved ones. Through their recollections, Felicia Montealegre Bernstein's spirit continues to shine, reminding us of the indelible mark she left on the hearts of many.

53. The Maestro's Global Impact: Changing the World Through Music

Leonard Bernstein's influence extended far beyond the concert halls of America. His music, teachings, and humanitarian efforts resonated on a global scale, making him one of the most internationally recognized and celebrated maestros of his time.

Bernstein's tours with the New York Philharmonic took him to every corner of the globe. From the historic concert in the Soviet Union during the Cold War to performances in Latin America, Europe, and Asia, Bernstein used music as a universal language to bridge cultural and political divides. These tours weren't just about showcasing musical prowess; they were about fostering understanding and building connections.

In countries emerging from conflict or undergoing significant political transitions, Bernstein's concerts often served as a beacon of hope. His performance of Beethoven's Ninth Symphony in East Berlin, shortly after the fall of the Berlin Wall, stands as a testament to music's power to heal and unite. The concert, attended by thousands, symbolized the breaking of barriers and the promise of a united future.

Bernstein's commitment to global education was equally impactful. Through television broadcasts like the "Young People's Concerts," he introduced classical music to millions worldwide. These programs, translated into multiple languages, demystified complex musical concepts and made them accessible to people of all ages and backgrounds.

His humanitarian efforts further solidified his global impact. Bernstein was a vocal advocate for nuclear disarmament, civil rights, and the end of apartheid in South Africa. He believed in using his platform to champion causes close to his heart, often intertwining music with activism. The concerts for peace, which he organized in various global hotspots, raised awareness and funds for numerous humanitarian causes.

Artists and musicians worldwide have spoken of Bernstein's influence on their careers. His innovative techniques, passionate approach to conducting, and commitment to mentorship have inspired generations of performers. Many of today's leading conductors and composers cite Bernstein as a pivotal figure in their musical journey.

Leonard Bernstein's global legacy is multifaceted. He was not just a maestro but a global ambassador for music, peace, and understanding. Through his art and actions, he showcased the transformative power of music, leaving a lasting impact on communities, artists, and music lovers worldwide.

54. Felicia's Influence: Her Role in Bernstein's Success

Behind every great individual, there often lies a pillar of strength, support, and inspiration. For Leonard Bernstein, that pillar was his wife, Felicia Montealegre Bernstein. While Leonard's genius was undeniable, Felicia's influence on his life and career played a pivotal role in shaping the maestro's journey.

Felicia, an accomplished artist in her own right, brought a unique perspective to Leonard's world. Her deep understanding of the arts, combined with her intuitive grasp of human emotions, provided Leonard with invaluable insights. They often engaged in profound discussions about music, performance, and the essence of art, refining and enriching Leonard's ideas.

Beyond intellectual companionship, Felicia offered unwavering emotional support. The world of music, with its highs and lows, can be tumultuous. Felicia was Leonard's anchor during challenging times, offering encouragement, understanding, and love. Her belief in his talent and vision bolstered his confidence, pushing him to explore new horizons and take bold risks.

Their home became a hub for artists, intellectuals, and musicians. Felicia's grace and charm made their gatherings legendary. These interactions, facilitated by Felicia's innate ability to connect with people, exposed Leonard to diverse perspectives, further broadening his musical horizons.

Felicia's influence extended to Leonard's compositions as well. Her passion, her struggles, and her essence found their way into Leonard's music. Pieces like "Symphony No. 2: The Age of Anxiety" carry traces of their shared experiences and emotions. Felicia was not just a muse; she was a collaborator in the truest sense.

However, their relationship wasn't without challenges. The pressures of fame, Leonard's demanding schedule, and personal struggles tested their bond. Yet, through it all, Felicia's resilience and commitment to their love story shone through. Her letters to Leonard, filled with raw emotion, reflect the depth of their connection and the mutual respect they held for each other.

In Leonard Bernstein's illustrious career, Felicia's influence is evident at every turn. Her role, both subtle and profound, shaped the maestro's life in countless ways. Through their shared journey, Felicia Montealegre Bernstein emerged not just as Leonard's partner but as a driving force behind his unparalleled success.

55. The Maestro's Farewell: Final Thoughts and Moments

The final chapter in Leonard Bernstein's life was as profound and impactful as the many that preceded it. As the curtain began to draw on his illustrious career, Bernstein's final moments were filled with introspection, gratitude, and a deep sense of purpose.

In the twilight of his life, Bernstein's health began to wane, but his spirit remained undiminished. He continued to conduct, teach, and engage with music, showcasing the same passion and vigor that had defined his career. Every performance, every lecture, was imbued with a sense of urgency, as if he was trying to impart as much of his knowledge and love for music as he could in the time he had left.

His final concerts were emotional affairs, not just for him but for the audiences that had come to love and respect him over the decades. There was a palpable sense of history being made, of witnessing the end of an era. Bernstein, ever the showman, ensured that these performances were memorable. His choice of pieces often reflected his own journey, his struggles, and his hopes for the future of music.

Away from the limelight, Bernstein spent his final days surrounded by family and close friends. These moments were filled with reminiscing, music-making, and deep philosophical discussions. Bernstein, always the teacher, continued to mentor and guide young musicians, passing on his wisdom and experiences.

His final interviews and writings provide a window into his soul. They reveal a man at peace with his legacy but concerned about the future of classical music. He spoke candidly about his fears, his regrets, and his hopes. He expressed a deep desire for music to continue being a force for good, for it to inspire and heal future generations.

Bernstein's passing in 1990 marked the end of an era. The world mourned the loss of a musical titan, a visionary, and a beloved teacher. Tributes poured in from all corners, reflecting the global impact of his life and work.

Yet, in death, as in life, Bernstein's influence endures. His music continues to inspire, his teachings resonate, and his legacy stands as a testament to a life well-lived. Leonard Bernstein's farewell was not a goodbye but a passing of the baton to the next generation, ensuring that his spirit and vision would continue to shape the world of music for years to come.

56. Felicia's Lasting Love: Her Enduring Bond with Bernstein

The narrative of Leonard Bernstein's life is incomplete without acknowledging the profound influence and unwavering support of his wife, Felicia Montealegre Bernstein. Even after her untimely passing in 1978, her presence remained a guiding force in Bernstein's life, a testament to the depth and strength of their bond.

Felicia and Leonard's relationship was a confluence of two artistic souls. Their shared passion for the arts, combined with mutual respect and admiration, laid the foundation for a love story that would withstand the test of time. They navigated the complexities of fame, personal challenges, and the ever-evolving landscape of the arts together, drawing strength from each other.

After Felicia's passing, Leonard often spoke of the void she left behind. He would reminisce about their shared moments, their intellectual discussions, and the quiet moments of introspection they enjoyed together. It was evident to those close to him that Felicia's memory was a source of both solace and inspiration.

In his compositions and performances following her death, subtle tributes to Felicia could be discerned. Whether it was a melancholic melody or a poignant phrase, Leonard's music became a canvas on which he painted his grief, love, and longing. Pieces like "Kaddish" Symphony, which he dedicated to her, encapsulated the myriad emotions he felt in her absence.

Leonard's personal letters and journals from this period provide a deeper insight into his emotional state. They reveal a man grappling with loss, trying to find meaning and purpose in a world without his muse. Yet, amidst the sorrow, there's a recurring theme of gratitude – for the years they shared, the memories they created, and the love that continued to blossom even in her absence.

Friends and colleagues often remarked on Leonard's resilience during this period. While he deeply mourned Felicia, he also celebrated her life, ensuring that her legacy lived on. He spoke of her achievements, her passions, and her unwavering commitment to the arts, ensuring that the world remembered her not just as Leonard Bernstein's wife but as a remarkable individual in her own right.

As the years passed, Felicia's influence on Leonard remained undiminished. She became a beacon of hope, guiding him through challenging times and inspiring some of his most profound works. Their love story, filled with highs and lows, passion and pain, serves as a testament to the enduring power of love, transcending the boundaries of life and death.

57. The Maestro's Mark: How Bernstein Changed Music Forever

Leonard Bernstein's impact on the world of music is immeasurable. His contributions spanned genres, bridged cultures, and inspired generations. As a conductor, composer, educator, and advocate for the arts, Bernstein's legacy is a testament to his unparalleled talent and vision.

From the concert halls of New York to the classrooms of Harvard, Bernstein's influence was felt everywhere. His ability to blend classical traditions with contemporary sounds revolutionized the way audiences perceived music. He wasn't just a maestro on the podium; he was a force of nature, pushing boundaries and challenging conventions.

As a composer, Bernstein's works are a reflection of his diverse influences and eclectic tastes. From the jazzy rhythms of "West Side Story" to the haunting melodies of "Chichester Psalms," his compositions are a testament to his versatility and genius. He had an innate ability to capture the zeitgeist, making his music both timeless and relevant.

But perhaps Bernstein's most significant contribution was his commitment to education. He believed in the power of music to enlighten, inspire, and transform. Through his televised lectures, he introduced classical music to millions, demystifying complex compositions and making them accessible to all. His passion for teaching was evident in every lecture, every demonstration, and every performance.

Bernstein's impact wasn't limited to the United States. He was a global ambassador for music, using his platform to promote peace, unity, and understanding. His concerts at the Berlin Wall, his efforts to bridge the gap between the East and the West, and his advocacy for artists' rights are a testament to his vision of a world united by music.

His collaborations with other greats, from Aaron Copland to Stephen Sondheim, further solidified his place in the annals of music history. He was a mentor to many, nurturing young talents and ensuring that the next generation of musicians had the tools and knowledge to succeed.

Yet, for all his achievements, Bernstein remained humble. He was a lifelong learner, constantly evolving and adapting. He faced criticism with grace, always striving to improve and innovate. His resilience, combined with his talent, made him a beacon of hope for many, a symbol of what's possible when passion meets purpose.

In the decades since his passing, Bernstein's legacy has only grown. His recordings are still revered, his compositions continue to be performed, and his teachings inspire new generations. Leonard Bernstein didn't just change music; he transformed the way we experience, understand, and appreciate it. His mark on the world of music is indelible, a testament to a life dedicated to the pursuit of excellence and the power of art to change the world.

58. Felicia's Final Notes: Remembering Her Life and Legacy

Felicia Montealegre Bernstein, while often recognized as the wife of the legendary Leonard Bernstein, was a luminous figure in her own right. Her life, marked by artistry, compassion, and resilience, left an indelible mark on those who knew her and the broader world of arts and philanthropy.

Born in Costa Rica and raised in Chile, Felicia's early life was steeped in the rich tapestries of Latin American culture. Her passion for the arts was evident from a young age. As a young woman, she moved to New York City, where she pursued a career in acting. Her performances, both on stage and television, showcased her depth and versatility as an artist. Her beauty, combined with her talent, made her a sought-after actress, but it was her intellect and spirit that left the most lasting impression on her peers.

Her marriage to Leonard Bernstein brought together two kindred souls. While their love story is well-documented, Felicia's influence on Leonard's life and work cannot be overstated. She was his muse, his confidante, and his anchor. Their partnership, both personal and professional, was a testament to their shared values and vision.

Beyond her roles as an actress and a wife, Felicia was a dedicated mother, a passionate advocate for the arts, and a philanthropist. She believed in the transformative power of music and art and worked tirelessly to make them accessible to all. Her charitable endeavors, from supporting young artists to championing causes close to her heart, showcased her commitment to making a difference.

Felicia's battle with cancer was faced with the same grace and resilience that marked her entire life. Even in her final days, she remained focused on her family, her passions, and her legacy. Her passing left a void in the world of arts and in the hearts of those who loved her.

Today, Felicia Montealegre Bernstein is remembered not just as Leonard Bernstein's wife but as a remarkable individual who left a lasting legacy. Her contributions to the arts, her philanthropic efforts, and her unwavering support for her family and friends are a testament to her spirit. Her life, marked by love, art, and compassion, continues to inspire and resonate, a beautiful melody that lingers long after the final note.

59. Encore: The Lasting Impact of Leonard and Felicia

The story of Leonard and Felicia Bernstein is one of passion, artistry, and enduring love. Together, they navigated the complexities of fame, personal challenges, and the ever-evolving world of the arts. Their combined legacy is a testament to their individual talents and their shared vision.

Leonard, with his unparalleled genius in music, reshaped the landscape of classical music and Broadway. His compositions, performances, and teachings have left an indelible mark on generations of musicians and music lovers. His ability to bridge the gap between classical and contemporary, to make music accessible to all, and to use his platform to advocate for peace and unity showcased his vision and commitment to his craft.

Felicia, on the other hand, was a beacon of grace and resilience. Her contributions to the arts, both as an actress and a philanthropist, showcased her depth and versatility. Her unwavering support for Leonard, her dedication to her family, and her commitment to making a difference in the world of arts and philanthropy have left a lasting legacy.

Together, Leonard and Felicia Bernstein were a force to be reckoned with. Their shared passion for the arts, their mutual respect and admiration for each other, and their commitment to making a difference made them one of the most iconic couples in the world of music and arts.

Their legacy is not just in the music they created or the causes they championed but in the lives they touched. From the young musicians they mentored to the audiences they inspired, the impact of Leonard and Felicia Bernstein is felt to this day.

The story of Leonard and Felicia is a reminder of the transformative power of love and art. It's a testament to the idea that two individuals, with their unique talents and vision, can come together to create something truly magical. Their legacy, both individual and shared, continues to inspire, resonate, and captivate, serving as a beacon of hope, passion, and excellence.

As the curtains fall on their story, the encore is clear – the music, the love, and the legacy of Leonard and Felicia Bernstein will continue to play on, touching hearts and souls for generations to come.

60. Curtain Call: Reflecting on Two Remarkable Lives

As the final notes of a symphony linger in the air, evoking a myriad of emotions, so too does the legacy of Leonard and Felicia Bernstein. Their lives, intertwined in a dance of love, art, and passion, have left an indelible mark on the world, resonating with those who have been touched by their stories.

Leonard Bernstein, the maestro of music, whose genius spanned the realms of classical, Broadway, and beyond, was a force of nature. His fervor for music, his innovative approach to compositions, and his ability to communicate the essence of a piece to audiences worldwide made him a legend in his own time. But beyond the accolades and the fame, Leonard was a man driven by a deep love for music and an unwavering belief in its power to unite, inspire, and transform.

Felicia Montealegre Bernstein, with her elegance, grace, and unwavering spirit, was more than just a muse to Leonard. She was a talented actress, a dedicated philanthropist, and a pillar of strength in the Bernstein household. Her influence on Leonard, both personally and professionally, was profound. Her own contributions to the arts and her dedication to charitable causes showcased a woman of depth, compassion, and resilience.

Together, they navigated the tumultuous waters of fame, personal challenges, and societal expectations. Their love story, filled with highs and lows, is a testament to their shared vision and mutual respect. Through the challenges they faced, both individually and as a couple, they remained steadfast in their commitment to each other and their shared passions.

As we reflect on their remarkable lives, it's evident that Leonard and Felicia Bernstein were more than just two individuals. They were a symphony, each note perfectly complementing the other, creating a melody that was both beautiful and enduring. Their legacy, both in the world of music and beyond, is a testament to their talent, vision, and dedication.

The curtain may have fallen on their earthly lives, but their impact continues to reverberate. Their story serves as a reminder of the transformative power of love, art, and passion. It's a testament to the idea that two individuals, with their unique talents and vision, can leave a lasting legacy that continues to inspire, captivate, and resonate.

As we take a moment to reflect on the remarkable journey of Leonard and Felicia Bernstein, we are reminded of the beauty of life, the power of love, and the enduring magic of music. Their lives, their love, and their legacy will forever remain a source of inspiration, a beacon of hope, and a testament to the transformative power of art.

Printed in Great Britain
by Amazon

35363384R00137